Fifty Favourite Wet Flies

T. Donald Overfield

Fifty Favourite Wet Flies

with illustrations by the author

A & C Black · London

First published 1986 by
A & C Black (Publishers) Limited
35 Bedford Row, London WC1R 4JH

Overfield, T. Donald
    Fifty favourite wet flies
    1. Trout fishing   2. Fly fishing
    I. Title
    799.1'755   SH687
    ISBN 0-7136-5565-8

Printed and bound in Great Britain by
Billing & Sons Limited, Worcester

Contents

Foreword

This 'Fifty Favourite' series is becoming a pleasant habit. Starting with *Fifty Favourite Nymphs*, followed by *Fifty Favourite Dry Flies*, I now put before you *Fifty Favourite Wet Flies*.

The choice of wet flies to be included in this book posed a considerable problem because the range is tremendously wide. Firstly, I had to decide in my own mind what constitutes a wet fly. I took the arbitrary decision to concentrate on what I can only describe as 'true' wet flies, flies that in their overall configuration present a shape that our forefathers would have recognised instantly. I have attempted to mix old and new patterns but by the very nature of the selection method there must be a preponderance of old flies, some of which may be totally unfamiliar to you; however, they are all past and present favourites.

As in the previous books in this series no attempt has been made to instruct the reader in the craft of fly tying because such is not the primary aim. Rather I have attempted to bring to you the history of the flies — what my late American friend, Arnold Gingrich, called 'The Perfume of the Charm'.

I have no doubt many experienced fly tyers may quarrel with my basic illustrations where I show 'beard' hackles as opposed to fully-wound hackles. This is a personal choice and there are no hard and fast rules, the decision is yours. The same applies to the stage at which some of the wings are tied in. Use whatever method you prefer.

I sincerely hope that within these pages you will discover some wet flies that are to your liking and which provide you with capital sport.

T. Donald Overfield
Solihull, Warwickshire

1 Heckham Peckham

Murdoch

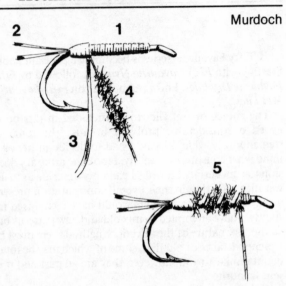

In his original *Trout Flies: A Discussion and a Dictionary*, Courtney Williams in 1932 expressed the view that this fly was not as popular as it was in the late nineteenth century, while in his updated edition of 1949, entitled *A Dictionary of Trout Flies*, he expressed the hope that the fly might some day come into its own again. If my postbag is an indicator I suggest that day is not far distant because a considerable number of still-water anglers have told me they find this old fly good medicine. First tied in the 1860s by an Aberdeen angler, named William Murdoch, the fly in various forms was highly popular for trout and sea-trout, both in Scotland and the rest of the British Isles. Its fame spread to Canada and America and between the two world wars the Heckham Peckham was prominently featured in most of the catalogues of the tackle houses over there.

Courtney Williams indicates a body of red seal's fur as his favourite version of this fly; however, I much prefer to stick to Murdoch's original pattern, especially when I venture north of the border. I have also found the true

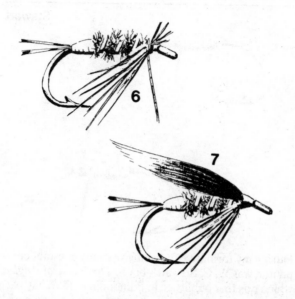

dressing to be equally acceptable to still-water trout; so
much so that a few years ago I gave a few Heckham
Peckhams to a number of my Midland flyfishing friends,
without telling them that it was an old fly, but simply ask-
ing them to let me know what success they had with the
fly. The result was quite startling, certainly vindicating
Murdoch's original idea. Try it for yourself because I am
sure you will find it a capital pattern.

For brown and rainbow trout the hook size is generally
10 to 14. Place the hook in the vice and wind the brown
tying silk to the bend (1), tying in two or three fibres of
pheasant tippet (2). Now tie in a length of flat silver tinsel
and wind as a tag (3). Wax the silk and dub with hare's
ear fur (4), winding to form the body and rib with open
turns of the silver tinsel (5). Tie in a beard hackle of red
cock hackle fibres (6). Finally tie in two wings from the
dark bluish-green white-tipped mallard feather (7). Complete the fly with a neatly whip-finished and varnished
head.

2 Red Spider

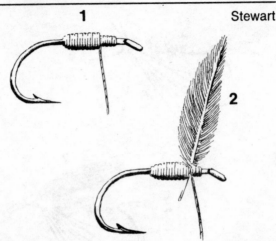

During my formative flyfishing years my constant companion was W. C. Stewart's book, *The Practical Angler*, which was first published in Edinburgh in 1857. My particular copy, dated 1919, became awfully dog-eared through constant reference and yet so many years later I still take it from the shelf and re-read it with affection, and for instruction.

Stewart wrote one of the most solidly informative books ever to be published on upstream wet fly fishing. In fact, that great angling historian J. W. Hills in his book, *A History of Flyfishing for Trout*, stated that Stewart was one of the four most influential men in the whole history of angling. The book was constantly in print from the first edition of 1857 right through to 1927 — a sure indication that what Stewart had to say was of importance to generations of anglers. Of course much of his advice on tackle is now old hat, though it is interesting to note that when 14-foot rods for trout fishing were quite usual he was advocating 10-foot rods. It is in the area of upstream wet fly fishing and fly tying that his comments of 1857 are equally relevant today. A staunch advocate of the sparsely dressed fly with the short Clyde-style body, he writes with clarity and authority on this subject and I

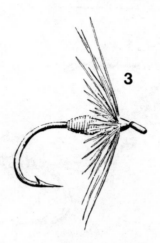

urge you all to find a copy of his book.

Never a man to load his fly-box with a multitude of patterns he specifies only three spider types – the Black Spider, the Red Spider, and the Dun Spider. In my youth the Red Spider could always be found in my tobacco tin and today, whenever I fish the tumbling broken water streams, I am happy to put a Red Spider on the point and fish it with total confidence. The tying is easy, though for maximum effect the fly must be sparsely dressed.

Put the hook (between 14 and 12) in the vice and take the yellow waxed silk in close even turns to a point no more than half way down the shank. Return the silk in tightly pressed turns back up the shank to form the body (1). Tie in a sandy red hen hackle (2) and wind around the forward bed of silk (3). The original pattern specified a small feather taken from the outside of the wing of a land-rail. Under no circumstances should we now condone the killing of this rare little bird and so you must use the substitute. Complete the fly with a neatly finished head.

Wherever tumbling waters foam and gurgle over rocky beds this simple little fly can be fished, upstream or down, with real confidence.

3   Claret and Mallard

Murdoch

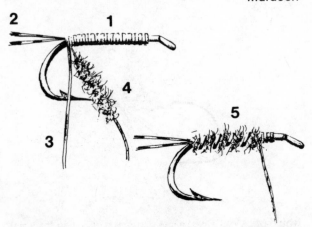

The first fly to have been described in this book was William Murdoch's excellent pattern, the Heckham Peckham. Now we come to the second fly reputedly from the vice of this nineteenth-century Aberdeen angler who seems to have had the knack of devising flies which, unlike many present day creations, stand the test of time.

Courtney Williams considered the Claret and Mallard to be one of the most universally popular wet flies extant, and I must agree with him. It is an excellent trout taker on lochs, modern still-water locations and rivers of all kinds. It is equally good for sea-trout when tied on a selection of larger hooks and I have known the fly to be good medicine for salmon anglers. Williams also suggested that the success of the pattern was because of its nymph-suggesting qualities; however, I have never been sold on this view, preferring to use a true nymph when trout are obviously feeding on natural nymphs. I do not pretend to know what old Murdoch had in mind when he devised this pattern but I have always thought of it as a represen-tation of a small fish. Certainly its ability to take trout has ensured it a place in my fly-box down the years and I would no more dream of fishing a highland loch without a Claret and Mallard in my team of flies than I

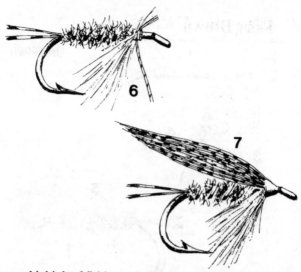

would think of fishing a chalkstream without an Imperial in my fly-box.

On one point Courtney Williams and I are in complete agreement and that is the colour of the body fur. To be really effective the body should be made from a very dark claret seal's fur, almost a dark ruby port colour. So many of the flies offered for sale have bodies ranging from bright red to dark scarlet. Do aim for a very dark claret colour.

For trout the usual size is between 10 and 14. Having placed the hook in the vice, wind the dark red silk down the shank to the bend (1) and there tie in a pheasant tippet (2), followed by a length of fine gold wire (3). Now well wax the tying silk and dub with the aforementioned claret seal's fur (4).

Wind the dubbed silk to form the body and rib with close even turns of the gold wire (5). Secure and remove waste dubbing and wire. Tie in a beard hackle of natural red cock hackle fibres (6). Secure and remove the waste ends. Take two slips from opposite feathers of dark bronze mallard (carefully marrying them together) and tie down as wings, well sloped over the body (7). Complete the Claret and Mallard with a neatly tapered head, well varnished.

4 Fiery Brown

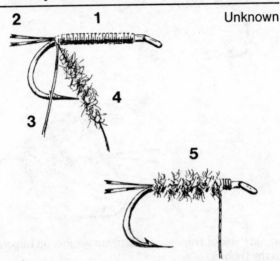

The name of the man who first tied the Fiery Brown is now lost in the mists of history and it is doubtful if we shall ever know who he was. The view has been expressed that the pattern can be traced directly back to the Bright Brown fly that Charles Cotton described in his contribution to Walton's book, though I think the point is arguable.

Of one thing we are sure: the man who popularised this pattern was Michael Rogan, 1833-1905, who lived in Ballyshannon, Ireland, and who was quite possibly the best fly-tyer the Emerald Isle has ever produced. Though his reputation rests mainly upon his superb salmon flies, his sea-trout and trout flies are worthy of their place in history. That eminent old writer, Francis Francis, pronounced that a Rogan fly was 'as like a piece of jewellery'. The sparkling brilliance he described was due to Rogan's dyeing techniques. In this sterile clinical age the old boy would not be allowed to keep a water-butt of ass's urine in the garden but this was the liquid he used as his cleansing and bleaching agent prior to dyeing the furs. Not for Rogan the powdered and liquid dyes of some factory production; he used natural materials, such as lichens,

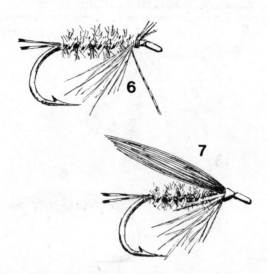

fustick, coppers and Brazil wood, to achieve the brilliance of his colours.

Again, I will quote Francis Francis describing the body of a Rogan tie: 'This is a difficult colour to describe as it is neither claret nor red, nor purple, nor puce, nor mullberry, nor mauve; it is more the old fashioned colour called Lake'.

Having presented you with the problem of matching Rogan's brilliance, I now leave you to your own devices. I doubt if your local council will allow a butt full of urine in your garden, but do your best!

The hook size for sea-trout is between 6 and 10. For browns or rainbows I suggest 12 to 14. Start the claret tying silk down the shank (1), and at the bend tie in a pheasant tippet for the tail (2), followed by a length of gold wire (3). Wax well the tying silk and dub with reddish-brown seal's fur (4). Now wind the dubbed silk to form the body and rib with the gold wire (5). Remove the waste. Tie in a bunch of red cock hackle fibres (6), securing and removing the waste. The wings are made from two slips of bronze mallard feather (7). Complete the fly with a whip-finished head and a neat coat of varnish.

15

5 Bloody William's Other Mate

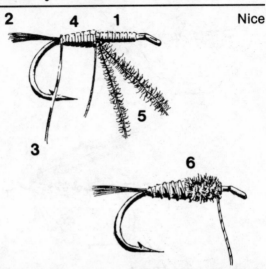

For more years than I care to recall, I have been in regular communication with a man who, in my experience, is certainly in the top five fly-tyers that I have ever known; and I venture to suggest that I am not exactly lacking in the ways of telling a superb fly-tyer from a very good one.

Jim Nice is one of those rare birds who has never advertised his wares, has never written an article or book on the subject and yet is never short of work from his regular clients who have long known the worth of a Nice fly. My admiration for Nice is not because he is a neat and meticulous tyer — countless others fall into that category. Rather it is because of his unique methods of tying the various stages, techniques that are not generally found in any book on fly-tying, and it is our joint hope that before Nice is too old to twirl a hackle, and I too old to pound a type-writer, we shall set down his tying methods for the enlightenment of future fly dressers.

This pattern of his own devising is mainly a sea-trout fly, containing to Nice's eye the prime colours, black, red and silver for a fly destined to catch that excellent fish. He has proved its worth countless times on his native river Axe, while his regular customers have found it to be

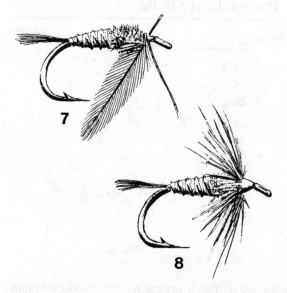

7

8

equally effective on waters the length and breadth of Great Britain. My own excursions after sea-trout are limited; however, it has worked well for me, also when chasing still-water rainbows.

I shall describe the tying of the fly in the usual dressing style, leaving Nice's special tricks and twirls for the book we have long promised we would write. For sea-trout the usual hook size is 12, but the pattern is equally effective for browns and rainbows over a wide range of hook sizes. Having placed the hook in the vice take the black tying silk down the shank (1) to the bend, and there tie in a tail of red dyed swan fibre (2). Nice's original had Ibis, now unobtainable. Having secured the tail, tie in a length of oval silver wire (3). Wind the silk back up the shank to the half-way mark (4), and there tie in a length of black ostrich herl (5). Bring your silk to the front of the shank, followed by the herl, tying in and removing the waste ends. Now take close even turns of the silver rib all the way up the body (6). Tie in a soft fibred black cock hackle (7), and wind around the shank in the usual way (8). Complete the fly with a neatly varnished head.

6 Parmachenee Belle

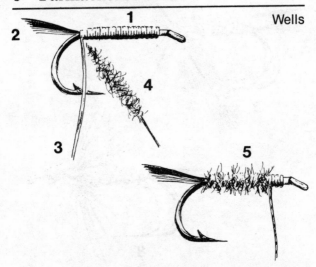

The invention of an American named Henry Parkhurst Wells, this fly has caused quite a lot of speculation down the years as to its date of origin. Our own angling historian Courtney Williams considered it to have been tied 'a few years before 1880', while the American Historian, J. Edson Leonard, indicates 'about 1885'. I think Williams was nearer the mark, for recent evidence points to the early 1870s.

H. P. Wells was a lawyer who lived in Brooklyn, New York, and he was also a writer with three books to his credit: *Fly Rods and Fly Tackle* (1885), *The American Salmon Fisherman* (1886) and *City Boys in the Woods* (1890). He frequently made the undoubtedly arduous trip from Brooklyn to a fishing location called Camp Caribou on the banks of lake Parmachenee in the county of Maine. A contemporary journal stated that the camp was eighteen miles from the nearest habitation and that it could easily be reached from New York in forty hours. One had to be keen in those days.

The gaudy colours of the fly have given rise to much discussion as to what the pattern represents. Let Mr Wells speak for himself: 'The trout take the fly not as an insect

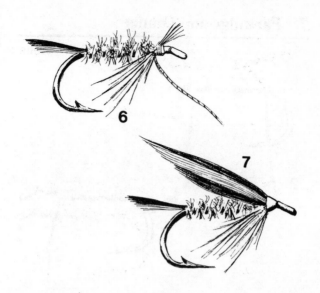

but as some form of live-bait. An imitation of some favourite food is in itself sufficient under all circumstances, provided it is so conspicuous as readily to be seen. To test this theory the fly in question was made, imitating the colour of the belly fin of the trout itself'. Had Wells got his tongue firmly in his cheek when he wrote this, or did he believe it? We shall never know. However, we do know that he devised one of the most popular wet flies ever to be used in that vast country.

The tying is not difficult, but do take care to marry the feather fibres in a neat fashion. For British waters I would recommend hook sizes between 10 and 14. Take the light brown tying silk down the shank in even turns (1) to the bend and there tie in a tail of married white and red dyed goose wing fibres (2), the scarlet uppermost, followed by a length of silver tinsel (3). Now dub the silk with lemon-yellow mohair (4). Wind the dubbed silk to form the body and follow with turns of silver ribbing (5).

Tie in a bunch of red and white cock hackle fibres (6) and secure. Now carefully tie in two wing slips of married goose feather fibre in a sequence of white, red, white (7). Complete with a whip-finished head.

7   Partridge and Orange

Unknown

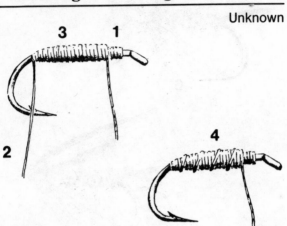

This has got to be one of my own favourite flies. As a Yorkshireman, could I say otherwise? All angling beginners in God's chosen acres are urged to believe in the unfailing power of the P. & O. and I still do. Where the rivers flow swift over rocky beds I will back this ancient fly against most modern creations. Cast upstream it has proved time and time again that the old folk knew a thing or two.

A propos de bottes, I wonder what those old Yorkshire anglers would think if they were to know that their county, which since Saxon times had been divided into three Ridings, the East, West and North, has now got a South Yorkshire and, by the stroke of a pen, my proud and ancient East Yorkshire has been reduced to North Humberside. What ill-conceived, misbegotten Whitehall department thought up that piece of nonsense? I flatly refuse to use such a name redolent of smelly mud-flats and broken fish boxes. In fact, I have a little rubber stamp which I thump onto the left-hand corner of all envelopes destined for East Yorkshire which states 'A pox on Humberside'.

I had better return to the subject of the Partridge and Orange before my blood pressure gets the better of me.

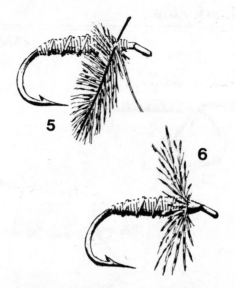

The pattern itself is as old as the hills and now no one can say with certainty what it represents. John Waller Hills in his very good book, *A History of Flyfishing for Trout* (1921), indicates that the pattern is an excellent representation of the blue-winged olive nymph, while others have put forward the view that it represents the February Red stonefly which is well known in the early months of the fishing season in the northern part of England. Certainly when the silk body of the artificial is well and truly soaked with water the silk takes on the beautiful mahogany shade of that natural.

Whatever it may represent I urge you to fish it with absolute confidence. Tie it on a size 14 hook, though I have also had cracking sport on a smaller size, 16. The tying silk (1) is unwaxed orange. Take it in close even turns down the shank to the bend and there tie in a length of very fine gold wire (2). Return the silk in close even turns up the body (3), and rib in close turns with the wire (4).

Now tie in a well-freckled feather from the back of a partridge (5) and wind round the hook shank, no more than two or three turns (6). Complete the fly with a well varnished whip-finished head.

8   Black Zulu

Unknown

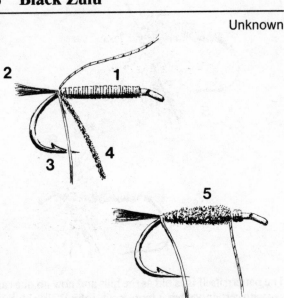

This simple effective fly has, I'm sure, been in existence for as long as man has fished with fur and feather, though I suspect the current name to be of relatively recent origin. The name Zulu smacks of the Zulu War, Rorkes Drift, etc., but I am only guessing. Can anyone help?

The basic dressing was certainly known to Thomas Barker, the first man to set out clear, concise fly-tying instructions in his book *The Art of Angling* (1651), for he writes of 'a black palmer ribbed with silver'. Charles Cotton, writing in the 1676 edition of Walton's book, is explicit: 'the Black Fly is made with a black body of the twirl of an ostrich feather, ribbed with silver twist, and the black hackle of a cock overall'.

No doubt there are other similar dressings, with minor modifications; however, let us get down to tying the Black Zulu as we know it today.

The hook size is usually between 10 and 14. Wind the black tying silk in close even turns down the hook shank

22

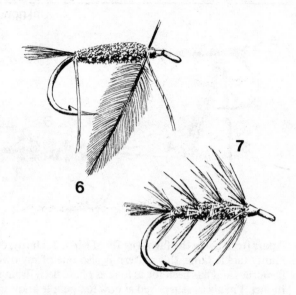

6

7

(1) until the bend is reached. There tie in a short tail of red wool (2) and a length of fine silver wire (3), and also a length of black wool (4). Some instructions specify black ostrich herl. I hate it, preferring wool.

Wind the wool to form the body (5) and secure with the tying silk, removing the waste wool. Now tie in a long black cock hackle at the front of the body (6) and carefully wind back in neat open turns to the bend. Maintain the tension on the hackle and, with precision, wind the silver ribbing up through the hackle to the head of the fly, securing the turns of hackle en route (7). Trap the wire under a neatly completed whip-finish. Finally, tweak off the waste end of the hackle at the tail of the fly.

Variants of the Zulu include the Blue Zulu, the difference being a dyed blue hackle substituted for the black hackle, though some tyers do run both colours together down the hook.

I have always found this to be a very good wet fly for grayling in late October and through November.

Hardy

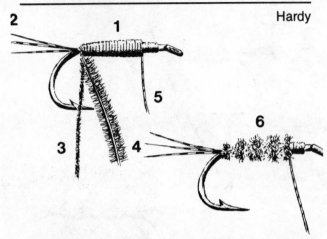

Apart from being the favourite fly of Mr J. J. Hardy, of Hardy tackle fame, this pattern is also one of my own favourites and has been for as long as I have been fishing. In fact, I'm always surprised at how few people know of it.

I was first introduced to this highly effective wet fly by an old gentleman in Northumberland when I was fishing the small river Allen close to that very pretty village of Allendale. The old boy had watched my slow and fishless upstream wading from the vantage point of a stone bridge that spanned the stream. Having reached the bridge, I clambered up the bank being in need of a dram from the flask and hoping to get some local knowledge of the ways of the Allen trout.

We fell to talking as we both contentedly leaned over the old stone wall, and I noticed his rod was set up and leaning against the hedge. He told me that, like many other anglers, as he advanced in age and knowledge his fly-box contained fewer patterns, until now he relied on no more than six patterns dressed in sizes varying from 16 to 12. He was also first and foremost a wet fly man who habitually fished a team of three or four flies, later demonstrating to me his casting with his old cane rod that had a set in it like a dog's hind leg. It would be a nice

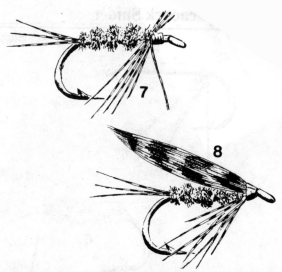

touch to the story if I were able to tell you that as he fished he took trout after trout. He didn't, and, as he later said, Saint Peter would have been hard put to take fish that day; however, he did give me a few of his Hardy Favourites and wrote down the dressing for me. Down the years we met again occasionally when both fishing the Allen, and he did prove to me what a good fly it was. He has now long been under the sod but I always remember him when I tie on a Hardy's Favourite.

I know that quite a few folk insist that the pattern is better known as a still water fly, yet I have had great success with this fly on rivers all over the land. I suppose it is a question of confidence.

The hook is generally 12 or 14. Take the brown tying silk in close turns to the bend (1) and there tie in brown mallard fibres (2) as the tail. Now tie in a length of thin red floss (3) and a strand of bronze peacock herl (4). Return the silk up the body to point (5). Wind the herl up the shank and rib with the floss (6). Secure and remove waste. Tie in a beard hackle of dark partridge fibres (7) and secure. Take two slips of dark brown turkey feather and tie as wings (8), sloping well back. Complete with a neat whip-finish.

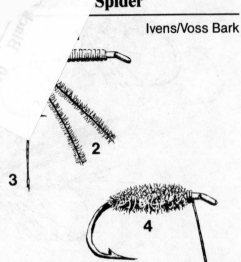

During recent correspondence with my friend, Conrad Voss Bark, we fell to discussing his favourite wet fly; any fly that Conrad approves of must be good, for his experience is tremendous. With little hesitation he plumped for the Ivens pattern, and his own variation of that fly.

The original was first described and illustrated in T. C. Ivens' book, *Still Water Fly Fishing*. The fly was evolved almost by accident for Ivens was fishing an alder, without a great deal of success. Being somewhat dissatisfied with any wet fly that incorporated wings, he took a pair of scissors and cut them off, leaving only the peacock herl body and black hackle. The fly started to take trout and so it was back to the fly-tying vice.

The original Ivens tie is quite simple. The hook size is between 8 and 12. Take the well waxed tying silk in close even turns down to the bend (1) and there tie in two or three strands of peacock herl (2). Twist the strands of herl around the tying silk (3) and wind together up the shank to form the body (4). Now tie in a black hackle (5) and wind for three or four turns (6), completing with a neatly varnished head.

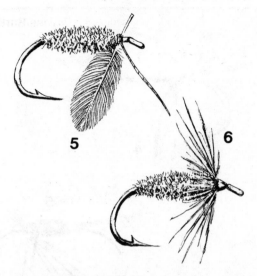

5

6

Voss Bark's version differs in being a shorter and smaller fly, and he now uses this almost to the exclusion of any other pattern when a spider type is called for. It is tied on hooks from 12 down to 16, and even 18. Conrad does not believe in using underlayers of wire to make the fly sink, preferring to have the artificial perform just below the surface, aiding animation by a few twitches of the line as the fly comes downstream, to 'work' the hackle.

I think I can do no better than quote from Conrad's letter to give you some idea of the pattern's effectiveness: 'I have fished the Black and Peacock Spider almost everywhere for trout, especially in late summer and autumn, on the chalk, limestone and spate rivers; practically always fished upstream and dropped down with a noticeable plop well above a fish or a place where a fish is likely to be. Sometimes the trout comes to it with such a splash you practically drop your rod. At other times they just suck it down as though they know beetles cannot escape'. Certainly a very good fly that you all should try.

11 Blae and Black

Unknown

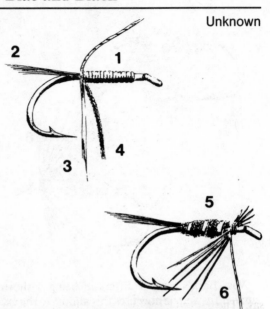

I confess that this fly is something of an enigma to me. Search as I may I have not been able to track down the name of the originator or a great deal about its history. The recognised historian, Courtney Williams, thought that it was of Irish extraction, though correspondence with fly-tyers in that country has not produced such evidence for me. The word 'Blae' is, I believe, Scottish and I would suggest that this fly is from north of the border. That the Blae and Black is usually dressed with a short 'Clyde-style' body tends to confirm this view, while in my collection of historic flies I have a beautifully tied example, dressed on gut. It is certainly pre-1860 and came from an old Scottish family. Again, the short body is in evidence. For my money, the Blae and Black is a Scot.

Prior to his death a few years ago the Scottish journalist, Tom Stewart, contributed a regular article to *Trout and Salmon* describing various flies and their tying. He described the Blae and Black as having a red tail, a piece of white feather dyed pillar-box red, and he went on to

say, 'The pattern I like best has a red tail . . . simply for the reason that I have a weakness for putting a red tail on many of the wet flies I use'. Now this does not tell us if he thought the original fly had a red tail, or that the fly was simply improved by such an addition.

I come down heavily on the side of the argument that says the original did not have a red tail and here Courtney Williams' description of the fly coincides with the old pattern in my collection, at least so far as the tail is concerned. In other areas there are slight variations. I prefer the old dressing.

The hook is size 14. Take the black tying silk in close even turns down the shank (1), but *not* to the bend. Stop half way down the shank. Here tie in fibres of golden pheasant tippet (2), followed by a length of silver tinsel (3) and a length of black wool (4). Wind the wool to form the body and rib with the tinsel (5). Tie in a beard hackle of black cock hackle fibres (6). Remove waste and secure. Tie on top a wing of starling wing feather fibre (7) and complete with a neatly varnished whip-finished head.

12   Shell Fly

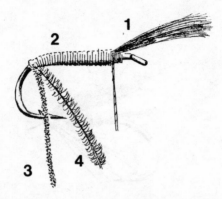

You will find no older instruction on fly patterns than those contained in *A Treatyse of Fysshynge wyth an Angle*, attributed to Dame Juliana Berners and published in 1496. Her patterns, twelve in all, are somewhat vague, lacking positive tying instructions and some historians are of the opinion that the patterns are not the Dame's original work but were culled from a much earlier French book; however, most are agreed that the patterns were derived from nature, being attempts to translate into fur and feather the form and colour of some natural insects.

Many years ago I attempted to follow Dame Juliana's somewhat difficult and ambiguous instructions, tying up a set of her flies as near as I could to the written word and materials in her description. Having completed the exercise, the flies were put into a box and forgotten. One day, when I was due to fish the Yorkshire Derwent that flows through Hackness, I rang my host to confirm our arrangements and as we talked the conversation drifted round to Juliana Berners and her flies. I remembered my tyings and agreed to bring them with me on my trip north.

The next day found us in the Everley Hotel having a pre-fishing dram and sorting out our fly-boxes, not least the twelve Berners patterns. As the next three days were

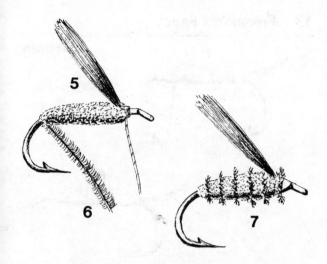

to be devoted to fishing, I did not mind making a fool of myself for the first day when my host suggested that I should fish only with one of the patterns, and he would choose it. He picked the Shell Fly for me to use. The trout were not in the best of tempers but, fished upstream and dropped under overhanging bushes with a decided plop, the old pattern did remarkably well. Since that day I usually carry a few Shell Flies, mainly to give to other flyfishers just for the pleasure of seeing the look on their faces when they hook a decent fish on a fly that was devised nearly four hundred years ago. Do try it.

Use a number 14 hook. Start the mid-green tying silk down the shank and tie in a slip of pale starling fibre (1). The original dressing called for 'bostarde' (bustard), now unobtainable. Continue the silk to the bend (2) and tie in a strand of green wool (3), followed by a strand of peacock herl (4). Wind the wool up the shank to form the body and bring the wing into a position so that it is sloping slightly rearwards (5). Wind the peacock herl (6) in open turns up the body (7) and in front of the wings, completing the fly with a whip-finished head. A word of warning: the fly is only good for one or two fish because the herl rib breaks very easily, but there again your trout may prefer a trailing rib!

13 Freeman's Fancy

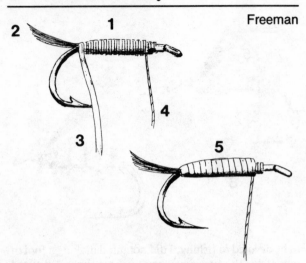

Though I may be putting my foot in it, I must say that there are times when I think that a great number of flyfishers who just fish the many and varied still-water locations up and down the country consider that the only sort of fly to tempt the rainbows must have been invented within the past few years, ideally by one of the big names in reservoir fishing. I know more than one or two who think that modern fisheries require modern fly patterns, being prepared to consider as rubbish flies that have their origins in the dim and distant past. I feel sorry for them.

Do not let me cause you to think that I am a complete red-necked reactionary who would never use a modern lure, for such would be equally foolish. I believe that modern fly patterns and lures all have a place, as my fly-box will show. However, I do sometimes wonder if in the rush and bustle of fly design advancement, modern materials, etc., many old and tried patterns tend to be overlooked, patterns that, if given a fair trial, would prove to be as effective as their modern counterparts. The Freeman's Fancy is a case in point and I have proved to my own satisfaction that this pattern is most attractive to the rainbows of the Midlands, though it was first tied

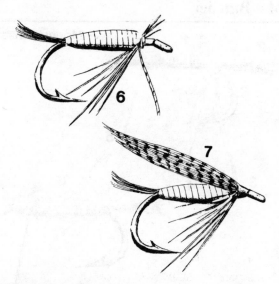

almost ninety years ago.

The invention of Captain W. Freeman (who lived in Oxfordshire) the Fancy was, I believe, originally intended as a sea-trout fly, though his frequent fishing trips to Scotland quickly proved it to be a capital loch pattern. In later years it came into its own at such locations as Chew, while it is on record that a regular angler on the loughs and rivers of Ireland took ninety percent of all his fish on this fly.

The tying is not difficult, but do take care with the proportions. The hook size is between 10 and 14, usually the larger size. Take the tying silk down the shank in close even turns (1), and at the bend tie in a tail of dyed orange swan fibres (2), followed by a length of flat gold tinsel (3). Return the silk to point (4). Wind the tinsel in even overlapping turns to form the body (5) and remove the waste. Tie in a throat hackle of cock fibres dyed a magenta colour (6), followed by wings of brown mallard married fibres (7).

The original pattern had a tail of orange coloured toucan feather; this is virtually unobtainable, unless you have a friend working in a zoo.

14 Butcher

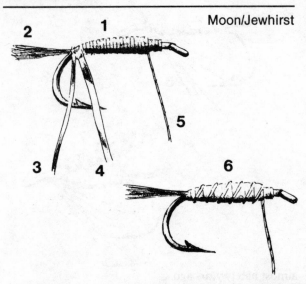

Here is a real old favourite beloved of countless anglers since it was first designed in the early 1800s. To my mind it epitomises the true wet fly: shiny, colourful and sleek.

Many anglers are under the impression that the Butcher hails from the lands of mist and heather, whereas it could hardly have come from an area further removed from Scotland, being devised in that most English of towns, Tunbridge Wells. One almost expects it to have been the invention of 'Disgusted of Tunbridge Wells'! Such was not the case: it seems to have been the joint effort of a Mr Moon and a Mr Jewhirst who lived in that town. Courtney Williams was of the opinion that the pattern was invented very early in the 1800s and was originally called the Moon Fly. I have been unable to find confirmation of this. Most historians seem agreed that the fly became known as the Butcher round about the late 1830s and one can see from the colours of the pattern that the new name suited the fly; the dark blue of the wings is close to the blue of the traditional butcher's apron, the vivid red tag approximates to the colour of freshly killed meat, while the sparkling silver can be related to the

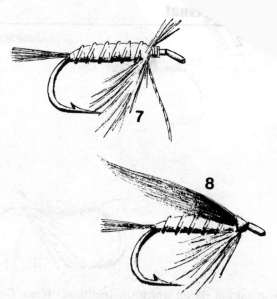

knives of the trade. Finally, Mr Moon was a butcher and so everything fits together very neatly. No doubt the fly's ability to slaughter trout contributed to the change of name, if such was the case.

As with most other flies of some antiquity there have been variations. Possibly the most well-known is the Bloody Butcher, which derives its name from the red hackle that replaces the traditional hackle.

The hook size varies between 10 and 14. Wind the black tying silk in close, even turns down the shank to the bend (1) and there tie in a short length of dyed red goose feather fibre as the tail (2). The original pattern specified red ibis. Now tie in a length of fine oval wire (3) and a length of flat silver tinsel (4).

Wind the flat tinsel in slightly overlapping turns to form a tapered body, followed by the rib of oval silver wire (6). Secure and remove waste. Now tie in a bunch of black cock hackle fibres (7) and secure. The wing is made of slips from the blue-black wing feather of the mallard, tied to slope well down over the body (8). Complete the fly with a neatly-tapered and varnished head.

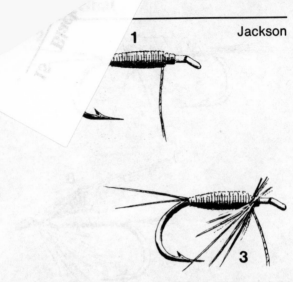

The natural fly on which the traditional Black Gnat dressing is based was long considered to be *bibio johannis* of the Diptera family; however, that top class entomologist and flyfisher, John Goddard, states that the term Black Gnat can be applied to many other natural flies, i.e. *scydromia glabricula, hilaria maura, dilophus febrilis* and the *simmulium* reed smuts. The average angler need not concern himself too much with the hairsplitting approach of the dedicated entomologist because most artificial representations are welcomed by the trout, whatever the naturals may be that are falling on the water.

But which artificial should one tie? The history of the Black Gnat is almost as old as the recorded history of our sport, while there seem to be as many different dressings as there are books on angling. Allowing for the fact that many early angling authors cheerfully stole one another's patterns, we are still left with a plethora of flies from which to choose. I will give you three only.

In 1676 Charles Cotton gave a dressing having a body made from the dubbed fur from the down of a young coot, or black 'water dog', while the wings were feather fibres from a mallard 'as white as can be'. In 1747 the

36

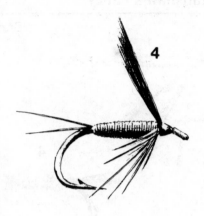

Bowlkers' book, *The Art of Angling*, gave a body of black ostrich herl, topped off with a dark blue hackle. R. S. Austin, of Tup's fame, gave a tying in his unpublished manuscript of 1890 having a body of purple silk ribbed with the greenish fibre from a magpie's tail, wings of sparrow fibre and a dark hackle.

But my own favourite tying of the Black Gnat was quoted by John Jackson, the author of *The Practical Flyfisher* which was published in 1854. The same dressing is also noted in Ewen Tod's very good book *Wet Fly Fishing* of 1903.

The hook is usually 16. Take the black silk down the hook (1) to the bed and there tie in two fibres from a black cock hackle as the tail whisks (2). Return the silk up the shank to form a tapered body and there tie in a bunch of black cock hackle fibres (3). Now take a small bunch of fibres from a young starling's wing feather, roll them together and tie in as the wing (4). Do not split into two with the silk but keep as a single wing in an upright position.

Go forth and fish this fly with confidence, and never mind the entomologists!

16 Bradshaw's Fancy

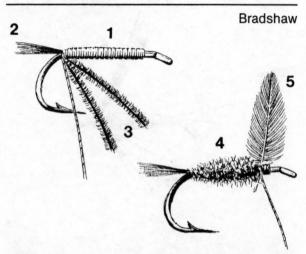

Many years ago I bought, for a truly trifling sum of money, a pristine second-hand copy of F. M. Walbran's book, *Grayling and How to Catch Them*, published in 1895. Having the good fortune to fish in good grayling country and, quite early in my fishing career, having come to appreciate the fighting ability and culinary quality of the winter fish, I read with great interest all that Walbran had to say on the matter.

I am sure that the poor opinion of grayling held by many anglers is based upon their experiences of hooking these lovely fish during high summer when they are at their lowest ebb. Hook the same fish in late autumn/early winter and you will wonder at their fighting ability and stamina. But now back to Mr Walbran and what he had to say.

Walbran lists, among others, twelve 'fancy' flies, patterns that bear no relationship to any natural insect but which have proved to his satisfaction, and the equal satisfaction of a number of his contemporary Yorkshire anglers, that such artificials were very good medicine for the winter fish. Down the years I have given most of the twelve flies a tryout now and again, but I come back every time to the one called Bradshaw's Fancy as one of my

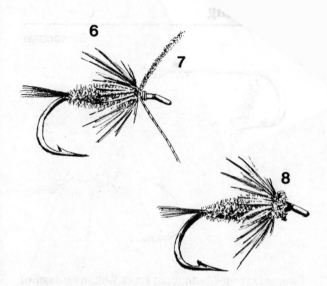

very favourite grayling patterns.

Devised towards the end of the nineteenth century by Henry Bradshaw of Bramley, near Leeds, it proved to be not only a good grayling fly but also a capital trout fly, for Walbran records that Bradshaw, who regularly fished the Yorkshire Anglers' Association water, Eamont, did with some regularity kill between twenty and thirty trout a day with this artificial.

I usually tie the fly on size 14 hooks. Take the dark purple tying silk in close even turns to the bend (1) and there tie in a tag of bright crimson wool (2), followed by two or three strands of copper-coloured peacock herl (3). Twist the herls together and wind to form the body, following with spaced turns of silk as ribbing (4). Secure and remove waste herl. The original dressing called for a hackle from the neck of a Norwegian crow. This feather is of a pale blue-dun colour and I suggest you tie in such a coloured hen hackle (5). Wind on the hackle and secure, removing waste end (6). Now tie in a short length of bright crimson wool (7) and wind for a couple of turns just in front of the hackle (8). Complete the fly with a neatly finished head.

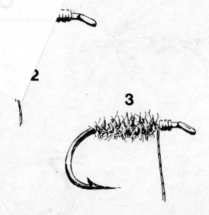

2

3

If you read the 1676 edition of Izaak Walton's *Compleat Angler* you will find Charles Cotton's dressing of a Cowdung fly. The remarkable fact is that since then subsequent patterns have altered but in detail, while the overall hue of the many artificials has stayed stable.

What is a natural Cowdung fly? It is *scatophaga stercoraria* and it takes its common name from the fact that the female lays her eggs in the excrement of cattle. Being a land-based insect, it is not seen in large numbers upon the water except when strong winds are blowing and the flies are carried onto the stream. In the early part of the trouting season water-born flies are often scarce and at such times a fall of cowdung (the insects, of course) can do much to liven up the trout.

A search through the old books on flyfishing quickly shows that this fly has held an important place in anglers' lists of flies over many generations. I will list but some of the books that carry the Cowdung dressing: Bowlker's *The Art of Angling* (1747), Salter's *The Modern Angler* (1811), Bainbridge's *The Fly Fishers Guide* (1816), Ronalds' *The Flyfishers Entomology* (1836), Shipley & Fitzgibbon *On Fly Fishing* (1838), Hofland's *The British Angler's Manual* (1837), Pulman's *Vade Mecum* (1841),

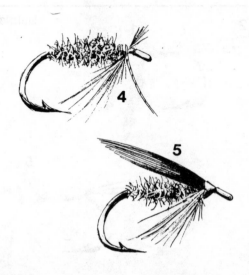

Blacker's *The Art of Angling* (1843), Beever's *Practical Flyfishing* (1849), Theakstone's *British Angling Flies* (1853), Ogden's *On Fly Tying* (1879) . . . the list is endless.

Having established that the little insect is well respected by all the great names in fly-fishing history, which pattern should you choose to tie? For my part I have always had a liking for the pattern described by Bainbridge in his book of 1816. The hook size can be between 14 and 16. Wind the yellowish-brown tying silk in close turns (1) down the shank to the bend. Wax the silk well and dub it with mohair of a subdued yellow colour (2). Bainbridge specified camlet as the material. A minute amount of brown fur can be added to the body dubbing, something I always do. Wind the dubbed silk to form the body (3), removing waste. Take a bunch of ginger hackle fibres and tie in (4). The original dressing called for wings made from the feather of the landrail, or corncrake as many know it, but you must now use a substitute material. I suggest that any feather fibre died a pale sandy-brown will suffice. Tie in the wings, sloping well back over the body (5), and complete with a neat head.

18 Half Stone

Unknown

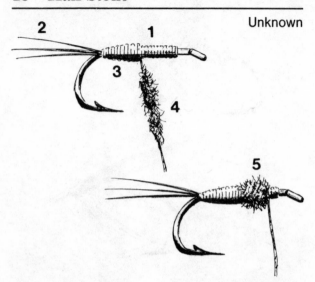

I confess that I have had little personal experience in the use of this wet fly, but as the word 'favourite' in the title of the book denotes not only my own favourite patterns but those of others also, then I am happy to include the Half Stone as being the first choice of a very old friend. The man in question is, alas, no longer able to cast to the trout or salmon because of old age and physical infirmity, but few things give me greater pleasure than to sit and listen to his needle-sharp reminiscences of the days just after the turn of the century and up to the end of the 1939-45 war.

That my friend lived and fished for the major part of his life in the border counties which divide England from Scotland makes his favourite fly a rather unusual choice because the Half Stone is something of a parochial pattern that has rarely found much favour outside the confines of its west country birthplace. It is a fly that must have appealed to F. M. Halford because, with suitable modifications, he changed it around to suit his dry fly code and it emerged as a full-blown floater in his book *Floating Flies and How to Dress Them*, published in 1886.

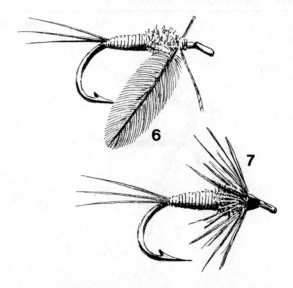

6

7

R. S. Austin, the west country inventor of the famous Tups, also gave a dry fly dressing of the Half Stone, though it differed considerably in having a body of bright yellow floss silk. For my money I accept the dressing given by Courtney Williams in *A Dictionary of Trout Flies*, it being the same wet fly dressing as used for many years by my old colleague.

The tying is quite easy. The hook can be between 12 and 14, though the latter is the usual choice. The waxed yellow silk is wound in even turns down the shank to the bend (1) where the tails of three strands of very dark natural blue-dun hackle fibres are tied in (2). Wind the silk back up the hook shank for half the length of the body (3). Now dub the tying silk with either mole's fur or water rat fur (4) and wind over the remaining half of the hook shank (5). Secure with a whip finish and remove waste material.

Tie in a sharp natural dark blue-dun cock hackle (6) and wind a maximum number of three turns around the hook shank (7). Remove the waste end and complete with a neatly tapered, well-varnished head.

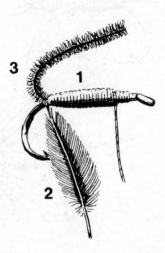

The county of Derbyshire and areas of the adjoining county of Staffordshire seem to have been breeding grounds for top-class fly-tyers down the ages. I'm sure that no other small area of the country can boast of such names as Charles Cotton, Frank and James Ogden, John Beever, Alfred Ronalds, Roger Woolley, David Foster, James Eaton, all excellent fly dressers, though it is to the Eaton family that we look for the background of the Bumble range of flies.

The Eaton family had a long tradition of fishing and fly-tying in the area of the river Derwent. Originally of Essex extraction the first George James Eaton, born in 1815, came to Matlock early in his life and established a reputation for his flies. He died in 1869 but left behind a son, also called George James, born in 1845, who is reputed to have devised the Bumble style. He died in 1901, leaving his son, yet another George James, to carry on the fly-tying tradition. With his death in 1931 the fly-tying attributes of the Eaton family seem to have been lost, unless some reader can give me additional information of

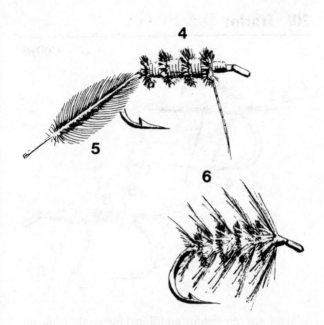

yet another George James?

Now we come to another famous Derbyshire angler and fly-tyer, David Foster, a member of the famous Ashbourne tackle-house which was founded in 1763. Foster's book *The Scientific Angler* (1882) was compiled from manuscripts left by him to his sons after his death. Foster had a high regard for the Bumble style of dressing and the pattern here described was one of his favourites.

The hook is generally a size 14. The pink tying silk (1) is taken along the shank to the bend and there is tied in a honey-dun hen hackle (2), followed by a strand of peacock sword feather herl (3) and a length of salmon-coloured floss silk. Wind the floss to form a plump body and secure. Rib the body with the peacock herl (4). Now wind the hackle (5) over the body and secure (6), completing the fly with a whip-finished head.

Roger Woolley (1877-1959) gives an alternative tie for the Honey Dun Bumble in his book *Modern Trout Fly Dressing* (1932) where he substitutes orange floss for the body, ribbed with ordinary peacock herl.

45

Collyer

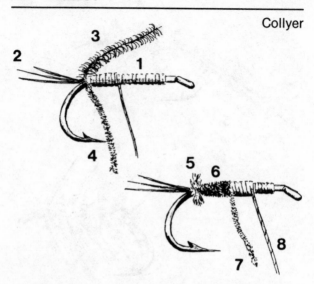

When I was researching additional material for the up-
dating of the fifth edition of Courtney Williams' classic,
A Dictionary of Trout Flies, I was in correspondence with
many fly-tyers and anglers. Over several months and after
receiving countless letters it became apparent that while
the development of new nymphs and dry flies had gone
on apace, the wet fly seemed to be the 'odd man out'. In
fact it seemed that the traditional style of the wet fly, as
opposed to lure design, was in the doldrums and had not
been the subject of a great deal of experimentation.

The exception to the rule was provided by David Collyer, a well-known fly-tyer whose book *Fly Dressing*
(1975) is highly readable. When I asked him to provide
me with dressings of his own most consistently successful
patterns, the Harlot came high on the list. He wrote that
it fulfilled two important criteria: it was most interesting
to tie, and it caught fish. An ideal fly for reservoir and
lake use, it should be fished on a floating line just below
the surface. Collyer also thought it to be at its best in the
evening. For my part I have caught many fish on this fly,
fully justifying David's opinions.

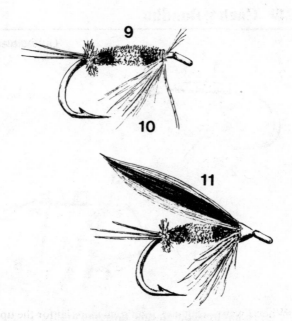

It is not easy to tie but, by the Lord Harry, how satis-fying when everything goes right! The hook is between 6 and 12. Wind the black tying silk down the shank to the bend (1) and there tie in a few strands of blue gallena fibres (2), followed by a length of peacock herl (3) and a length of black floss silk (4).

Wind the peacock herl to form a 'ruff'. Tie off and remove waste (5). Wind the tying silk forward for one-third of the body length. Now wind the black floss to form part of the body (6). Remove waste. Tie in a length of scarlet floss silk (7) and wind the tying silk for another one-third up the hook (8), followed by the scarlet floss (9). Tie in another piece of black floss and complete the body.

Tie in a bunch of blue gallena fibres as a beard hackle (10). Now comes the tricky operation: carefully 'marry' dyed goose feather fibres to give wings of a scarlet/black/scarlet configuration, and tie in two slips close over the body (11). Complete the fly with a neatly-tapered and varnished head.

21 Coch y Bondhu

Unknown

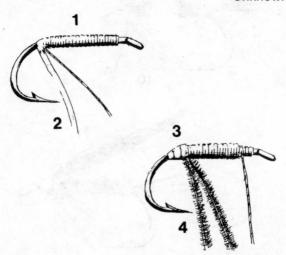

This just has to be the all-time favourite wet fly, though down the years the famous artificial has been known by many confusing names, e.g. Bracken Clock, Shorn Fly, Hazel Fly, Marlow Buzz, Fern Fly . . . one could go on. One can also get into fearful trouble over the spelling. Is it Coch y Bondhu? Coch y Bonddhu? Coch y Boldu? I have taken the coward's way out and opted for the usual spelling.

Just what does the artificial represent? A little beetle certainly, but is it *chrysomela populi* or *phyllopertha horticola*? Could it be *aphodius foetens*? Again, it might be *telephorus lividus*. All are put forward as contenders in Courtney Williams' classic book. I leave that one to the entomologists, though I do believe modern thought on the subject indicates *phyllopertha horticola*. Whatever the Coch y Bondhu represents, we all know it as a marvellous little chap when plopped under bankside bushes.

The traditional dressing is very well known, being two or three strands of copper hued peacock herl with a gold tinsel tag and a coch y bondhu hackle, that is, a deep natural red with a black list and black edges to the fibres.

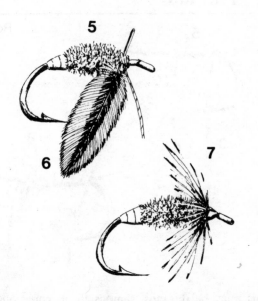

However, I am a great believer in a Coch y Bondhu pattern given by James Ogden in his book *Ogden on Fly Tying* (1879), where he states that the peacock herl should be tinted with magenta dye. Such treatment does give the herl a much richer hue. Just as an aside, Ogden also moans about the difficulty in obtaining good hackles of the correct colour. I quote: 'When I was a lad I could find this coloured bird at any barn door, but now you may travel a hundred miles and not see the right colour'. That was written in the late nineteenth century, but we seem to think the lack of decent hackles is a modern day problem. 'Twas ever thus!

But now to the tying. The hook size is between 12 and 14. Take the orange tying silk (1) down to the bend and tie in a length of gold tinsel (2). Wind the silk forward for a few turns, followed by the tinsel to form a tag (3). Now tie in two or three peacock herls (4), twist together and wind to form a plump body (5). Tie in a coch y bondhu hen hackle (6) and wind in the usual manner (7). Complete with a whip-finish.

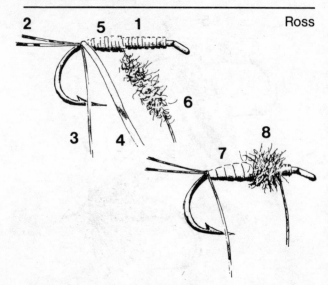

This must be the most famous fly to come out of Scotland. Known world-wide wherever anglers cast a fly to trout and sea-trout it has, by its very appearance, the look of a most effective killer. And yet this well-known pattern was not the brainchild of the man whose name it carries. In fact we do not know who first tied such a fly.

I think I had better explain. Peter Ross (1873-1923) was the owner of a small local general store in the village of Killin in Perthshire, Scotland. He was a keen angler and given to fishing the fly whenever possible. One of his favourite patterns was the traditional Teal & Red, but for some reason he fell to wondering how the old pattern could be improved. That he discussed the matter with a fly-tyer is certain, but who was that man? I would give a lot to know who first tied the fly to Peter Ross's instructions, changing the body to half-silver, half-red; and just why was the change made? Why not half-gold and half-red? Why not half-green and half-yellow? Sadly, we do not know the answer. However, one thing is certain: the chosen combination has proved to be mighty attractive to trout of all types, brown, rainbow and sea. Whatever the

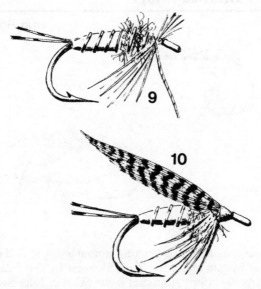

reason for the changes, the unknown fly-tyer and Peter Ross changed a good fly into a superb fly, and one that we can all fish with confidence.

For trout the usual size is from 10 to 14, while for sea-trout, hooks up to size 8 would not be unusual. The black tying silk (1), is taken in close, even turns down to the bend where a tail of golden pheasant tippet fibres (2) is tied in. Now tie in a length of fine oval silver wire (3) and a length of flat silver tinsel (4) at the rear of the shank. Wind the tying silk half-way up the shank (5), then re-wax the silk and dub it with red seal's fur (6).

Carefully wind the flat silver tinsel over the rear half of the body (7), followed by turns of the dubbed silk to form the forward half of the body (8). Take the fine oval silver wire and, with precision, rib in close even turns overall. Tie in and remove waste ends.

Take a bunch of black cock hackle fibres and tie in as a beard hackle (9). Secure and remove waste. Complete the fly with two matching slips of teal breast-feather fibre (10), tied low down for the wings. Finish off with a well-varnished head.

Swarbrick

Some years ago I was ferreting around trying to find out what I could about the Poult Bloa wet fly and I came across the information that it was listed in John Swarbrick's *Wharfdale Flies*, published in 1807.

I had never heard of Swarbrick or the list and this puzzled me, though I thought the matter could soon be clarified by going to my copy of Westwood and Satchell's *Bibliotheca Piscatoria*, that useful reference work for all who would collect angling books. I drew a blank, and neither was the book quoted in the supplement of 1901. Very strange. Swarbrick and his list of flies eluded me for months, when out of the blue arrived a small package from that knowledgeable book dealer, Ronald Coleby. On opening the packet I found a slim sixteen-page paperbacked booklet measuring only five inches by four inches. A real Tom Thumb book.

The title page states 'List of Wharfdale Flies by John Swarbrick (of Austby) 1807, and J. W. Sagar 1890'. The booklet was published in 1907 by Hemsley & Sons of Ilkley, Yorkshire, and has in bold letters the words 'Copyright: E. Beanlands'. The first nine pages are devoted to Swarbrick's patterns, the remaining pages listing those of Sagar. After the list of Swarbrick's flies, Mr Beanlands wrote, 'I conclude my extracts from this,

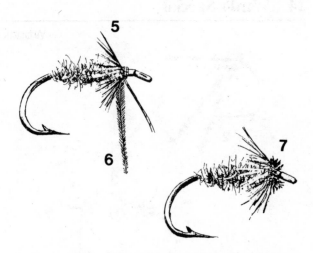

the . . . so far as I know . . . earliest monograph on Yorkshire trout fishing'. He may well have been correct.

What a little treasure this book is. Thank heavens the printers did not alter old Swarbrick's quaint spelling. Let me give you the flavour of it by quoting the dressing of the Knotted Midge: 'This Flie is very Small. A Hackle, the feather is taken from a Tuits [lapwing's] wing. The feathers lays near the Bodey. Harld [herled] at the Head with Magpie Feather. Drab Coloured Silk. The dark dawn [down] of a Hairs [hare's] Skut [the area under the tail] in the bodey'.

Since I first tied this pattern it has become a firm favourite of mine whenever small dark flies are on the water. I usually tie on a size 16 hook. Take the fawn coloured tying silk in even turns down to the bend (1). Now dub the silk with the under-fur from the hare's scut (2). Wind and form the body (3). The lapwing is protected and so you will have to ask a farmer or a keeper friend to keep a weather eye open for a bird that has died by natural causes if you wish to use the correct hackle (4), which is a very short soft-fibred feather. Wind the hackle (5), leaving plenty of room at the head to tie in a strand of magpie tail feather fibre (6). Wind on two or three turns of the herl (7) and complete with a whip-finish.

24 Ward's Special

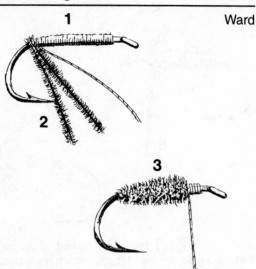

Many years ago a fellow Yorkshireman, T. K. Wilson, universally known to the angling world as Tim Wilson, had a series in the old *Angling* magazine in which he described his favourite flies and their history. For many years Tim was a regular contributor to a weekly column in the *Yorkshire Post*, writing under his well-known pen-name of 'Broughton Point'. Wilson's great loves were the rivers Aire and Wharfe which he described in detail in his book *Trout by All Means*, published in 1966 shortly before he died. In his *Angling* series he described a fly called the Ward Special, a pattern designed specifically for the limestone waters in the Malham area of Yorkshire and, in particular, for use in Malham Tarn.

The Tarn occupies a natural basin 1,300 feet above sea level in the Craven district and it is, I believe, quite unique because nowhere over its one hundred and fifty acres is it deeper than fourteen feet. For many years the water held excellent trout and, in fact, the quality of the fish is noted in a charter dated 1168.

The Ward Special was devised by Alfred Ward, under-keeper on the Tarn between 1882 and 1905, and then

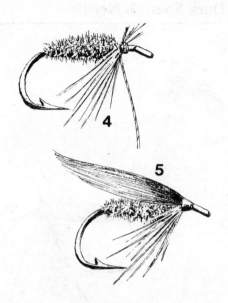

head-keeper until 1927. His pattern accounted for the best brown trout in 1924, a wild fish of 5 lb 14 oz. This is possibly not large by present day rainbow standards, but far more satisfying to catch than a stew-bred fish.

The Tarn, and the surrounding area, is no longer under private ownership for in 1946 it was handed over to the National Trust and later, in 1948, it was leased as a field study centre; however, day tickets to fish the Tarn are available if you contact the Resident Warden. On my last visit the midges were more in evidence than the trout, but sport was had on a Ward Special and the scenery is magnificent.

Now to the fly for which Tim Wilson had such a high regard. The hook can be between 10 and 14. The black tying silk is taken in close even turns to the bend (1) where two strands of dark peacock herl are tied in (2). Wind the herl to form the body (3) and secure. Tie in a bunch of black hackle fibres (4), followed by wing slips made from the tail feather of a magpie (5). Complete with a neatly whip-finished head.

Pritt

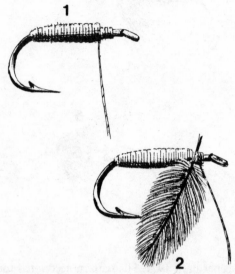

To find an artificial that generally represents the stoneflies which are found on many rivers and streams is not an easy task because, according to the entomologists, there are thirteen species, from the Large Stonefly of about 20 mm in length down to the Needle flies of about 8-10 mm.

Representations of the various natural flies have taxed the imaginations of many fly-tyers over the last few hundred years and the proliferation of patterns is large enough to make one's head spin. Most of the great names of our sport have put forward their own interpretations of the stoneflies. Blacker in *The Art of Angling* (1843) went so far as to differentiate between day and night patterns. Theakston, in his *British Angling Flies* of 1853, lists four alternative forms of winging, while Henry Wade in his *Rod Fishing with Fly, Worm and Minnow* (1861), lists a very different Spanish Needle. We can go even further back to the Yellow Sally of the Bowlkers in *The Art of Angling* (1747), or Ronalds' fly of the same name in his

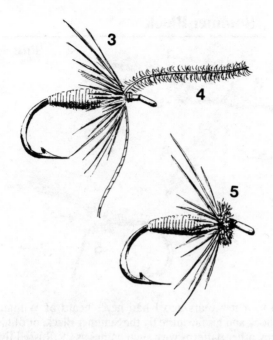

Fly Fishers Entomology of 1836. A little nearer the present day is the dressing of T. E. Pritt given in his *Yorkshire Trout Flies* of 1885, and it is this pattern that I use when needing such an imitation.

I tie it on hooks ranging from 10 to 14. Wind the orange tying silk in close even turns down the hook shank (1) to the bend, then return the silk, again in close turns, up the shank to form the body. Do not wax the silk prior to this operation for without the wax it turns a lovely mahogany colour when wet, just the effect we want. Now tie in a small feather from an owl's wing, the feather being located at the base of the wing (2). A suitable alternative would be a very small hen hackle of a light chocolate colour. Wind the hackle for two or three turns and secure (3). Tie a length of peacock herl in front of the hackle (4) and wind for two turns close up to the root of the hackle (5). Complete the fly with a neatly tapered and varnished head.

26 Summer Black

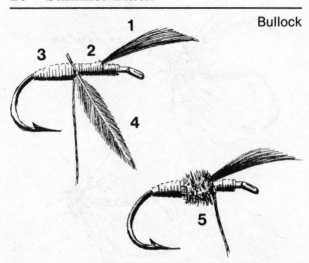

Up to a few years ago I had never heard of William
Bullock and his favourite fly the Summer Black, or of his
many other patterns with such names as the Russell fly,
Brandy Palmer, Stirtling and Lavender Black. They were
brought to my notice by that angling bibliophile and
dealer, Ronald Coleby, the man who introduced me to
the Knotted Midge described just a few pages ago. He
sent me another small booklet, via the post, entitled *Old
Bullock's Artificial Trout Flies*, and printed by J. H.
Wood in Macclesfield at a price of two shillings in the
year 1885. The little book contains a preface by a Mr A.
E. Parkinson, wherein he writes of 'the notorious
William Bullock'. Why notorious? I can only think he
must have been a very skilled poacher who earned the
grudging admiration of the more law-abiding anglers.
Can any reader shed some light on this matter?

The booklet contains seventy-one very original patterns, number forty-two being the Summer Black which,
it is stated, kills well from May to the end of the season in
all weathers, being best in 'full water of a porter colour'.
Who could resist trying out the favourite pattern of a
man called Old Bullock, who was also notorious to boot?

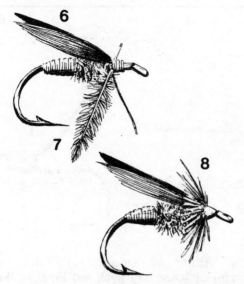

Being passionately interested in all that has gone before, I dressed up a few of the old lad's flies and on my next trip to the Dales his fly was offered to the trout. I cannot in all honesty say that it proved to be the touchstone for which we are always seeking; however, it did prove to be a very useful fly fished both upstream and down, especially downstream, for some odd reason, and I am now happy always to carry a few in my fly-box.

The tying is simple, but interesting. The hook size can be 12 or 14, though I usually go for the size 14. Start the crimson tying silk down the shank and tie in wing slips of starling wing feather (1). Continue the silk down the shank and trap the waste ends of the wing under the silk (2). Continue the silk to the bend. Return the silk in close turns half way up the shank (3) and there tie in a small rook quill feather (4). Bring the silk to the wing root and follow with turns of the rook feather (5).

Bring the wing into a rearward position (6), secure, and tie in a starling neck feather (7). Wind the starling feather close over the wing roots (8) and complete the fly with a whip-finished head.

Mold

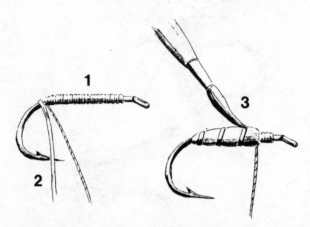

In 1967 Herbert Jenkins Ltd added to the welter of books
on flyfishing when they published Frederick Mold's
work, *Presenting the Fly to the Trout*. I have always
thought that this book did not receive the acclaim it
deserved and I would urge you to try to obtain a copy. I
hasten to add the usual disclaimer, for I have never met
Mr Mold, or written to him, though I'm sure either would
be an interesting experience. The author, like countless
others before him, developed a pattern to represent the
Hawthorn fly and to my way of thinking he came up with
a very good wet fly.

The Hawthorn fly, which, I have read somewhere, is
also called the Saint Mark's fly because the insect usually
puts in an appearance around St Mark's Day (which I
believe is the 25th April), has a limited period of hatching
and by mid-May one can usually forget about this small
creature. However, when the Hawthorn flies are blown
onto the water by the early season high winds the trout
love them and the flyfisher who is caught without a decent representation is at a distinct disadvantage.

Mr Mold states in his book, 'such a good mouthful is
never despised by the trout of either the river or lake and
happy is the prepared angler who notices that these

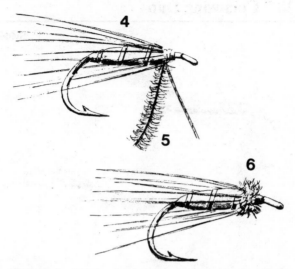

ungainly creatures are in the air when a likely wind is blowing'. He then describes the tying of his own pattern and goes on to say, 'This pattern, fished wet, has been responsible on many occasions for a complete abandon of caution on the part of the trout'. I agree with him and consider the pattern to be first class.

The tying is somewhat unusual but take some pains in the construction of this fly, and then go and fish it with confidence.

The hook size is usually 14. Wind the black tying silk (1) in even turns down to the bend and there tie in a length of fine silver or copper wire (2). Wind the silk back up the hook shank, followed by widely spaced turns of wire, and complete the body. Now clear varnish the whole body (3). At this stage Mold recommends that one should tie in a long-fibred black cock hackle and wind round the shank. I hope he will forgive me but I prefer to take a bunch of long hackle fibres and 'flair' them around the shank (4), the object of the exercise being to get the fibres laid well back along the body and to protrude beyond the bend. Now tie in a strand or two of black ostrich herl (5) and wind well over the hackle roots (6). Complete with a tapered and varnished head.

Foster

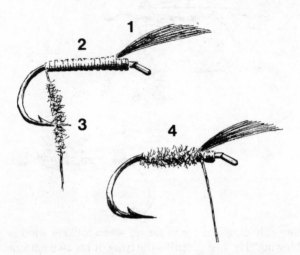

We have already examined a fly created by that knowledgeable Derbyshire angler, David Foster, when we looked at the Honey Dun Bumble, but he deserves more recognition for his patterns and fly-tying skills than the present day affords. Flies of his invention used to be firm favourites, a fact confirmed by many references in contemporary literature written by other well-known anglers of his time.

Readers will, I hope, forgive me if I inject yet another grayling fly into this book. I know that many of you may yet have to feel the electric thrill of a winter grayling on your line, but if my frequent references to this superb fish prompt you to understand that flyfishing does not end with the last day of the brown trout season and make you stir your stumps to go and find decent grayling water, then my objective has been achieved.

In 1888 T. E. Pritt's lovely volume *The Book of the Grayling* was published, and in that book are a number of excellent colour plates, one of which shows fifteen grayling flies, three each from recognized grayling anglers, Pritt included. Apart from the author there are

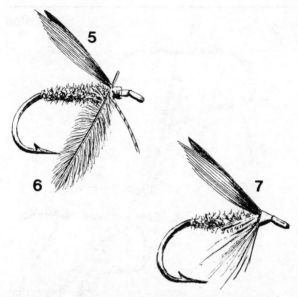

three flies each by Mr Walbran, Mr Bradshaw, Mr Lupton and Mr Foster. The latter's three flies are the Silver or Winter Dun, the Steel Blue Bumble and the Cockwinged Dun. Pritt states that the Cockwinged Dun is the only one that imitates a natural fly, and goes on to say that the artificial is the best, if not the only representation of a natural insect that is worth employing after the month of September.

Now to the fly. I usually tie it on a 14 or 15 sneck bend hook. Start the yellow tying silk down the shank and then tie in old starling wing fibres (1). Continue the silk to the bend (2) and dub the silk with water rat fur (3) very sparingly. Wind the dubbed silk to form the body (4). Now bring the wing back over the body at an angle of forty-five degrees (5) and secure. Tie in a blue-dun hackle freckled with yellow, or a light dun tinged with yellow dye (6). Wind the hackle in front of the wings and pull the fibres backwards and downwards, securing with turns of silk (7). Complete with a whip-finished and varnished head.

Rolt

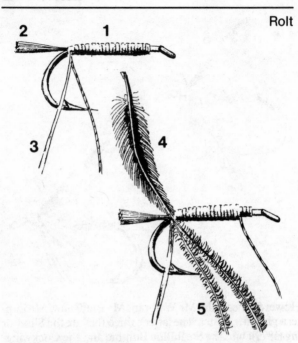

Readers may well think that I have an absolute fixation about grayling fishing for here is yet another pattern initially devised for the taking of those beautiful quicksilver fish. Readers may well be right, although this wet fly pattern has proved to be equally successful for trout, particularly when weighted with an underlayer of wire and fished deep for rainbows in still-water locations.

The Witch was a great favourite of the inventor, H. A. Rolt (not to be confused with James Rolt), the great fishing companion of G. E. M. Skues, who had a stile named after him on the Abbots Barton beats of the river Itchen. The Witch was described in Rolt's book *Grayling Fishing in South Country Streams* (1901) in the following manner: 'although I do not desire to blow unduly my own trumpet, I would rather pin my faith to an improved and glorified green insect I have discovered. It has been named the Witch and with it I have killed more grayling

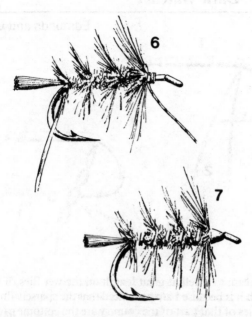

than with any other nondescript or natural I have tried, the Red Tag not excepted. As a wet fly it cannot be too highly recommended'.

I agree with Rolt's comments and, if dressed with a good cock hackle, it makes a very good dry fly. In general construction the fly is not unlike one of the Derbyshire Bumble family, though it is usually dressed on smaller hooks, 16 or smaller if your finger dexterity allows.

Take the green tying silk in close even turns to the bend (1) and there tie in a tail of bright red wool or floss (2). Now tie in a length of thin flat gold tinsel (3), followed by a honey-dun hen hackle (4) and one or two lengths of peacock herl (5). Wind the tying silk back up the hook shank, followed by the peacock herl. Secure and remove the waste ends. Now wind the hackle in open turns over the peacock herl (6). Secure and cut off waste. Maintain tension on the gold tinsel and carefully wind over the hackle stalk, trapping all in position (7). Complete with the usual neatly varnished head.

30 Dark Watchet

Edmunds and Lee

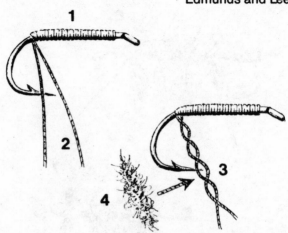

If I seem to dwell at great length on the wet flies of the north it is because I am convinced that the sparsely dressed flies of that part of the country are the epitome of the classic wet fly dressing. Nowhere is this more clearly expressed than in the Dark Watchet dressing described and illustrated in that classic work *Brook and River Trouting* by Harfield H. Edmonds and Norman E. Lee, published by the authors in Bradford in 1916.

Only ten years ago when browsing through a second-hand book shop I came across a mint copy of the book, price ten shillings! It was especially interesting because in a copper-plate hand on the flyleaf was written 'With Harfield H. Edmonds compliments'. The intervening years have shown a nice increase in value, for the book is now worth about £70. Though published in 1916 the quality of the colour photographs of the flies and the materials would put to shame many photographs reproduced in recent times. The text is equally interesting and I am delighted to see that a publishing firm was recently offering a modern reprint.

Illustration numbers 13A and 13B show two dressings of the Dark Watchet, or Iron Blue Dun, and how

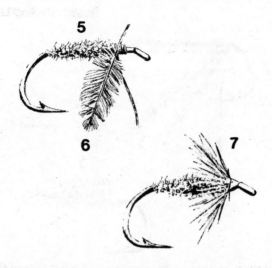

superbly they are tied. Of the two patterns I have always favoured dressing 13A, and I just cannot count the number of trout I have taken on this particular fly. I hasten to add that the general dressing was known long before Edmonds and Lee wrote their book: for example, Pritt gave the same tying in his *Yorkshire Trout Flies* of 1885; however it is a cracking fly.

The hook size is 16. Take the orange silk down the shank (1) to the bend and there tie in a length of purple silk (2). Now carefully twist the two strands together (3). Lightly wax and dub very, very sparingly with mole's fur (4). Alternatively, and this is not mentioned in the book, spread the fur along one of the silks, lay the other silk on top and twist together. I have found this traps the fur and allows the alternate colours of the silk to show through, this being an essential part of the overall body effect. Now wind the twisted silk and dubbing to form the body (5). Tie in a dark smoky blue feather from the throat of a jackdaw (6) or, alternatively, a similar coloured hen hackle, and wind in the usual manner (7). Complete with a whip-finish.

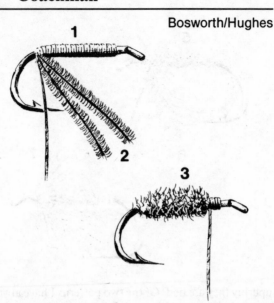

This particular artificial fly presents the historian with quite a few problems, not least the name of the person who actually invented the pattern, for we are reliably informed that in the early years of the eighteenth century the same fly was known as the Harding.

According to Courtney Williams, and despite an extensive search through my own reasonably comprehensive library, I have not found reason to doubt him when he says that the first reference to this pattern can be found in Salter's *Angling Guide*, the fifth edition of 1823. With slight dressing variations the fly is described in Hofland's *Anglers Manual* (1839), Kirkbride's *Northern Angler* (1840), and Fitzgibbons' *Handbook of Angling* (1847).

But who was 'the coachman' after whom the fly was named? It would seem there are two contenders for the title, Tom Bosworth and John Hughes. Bosworth was in the employ of royalty for most of his life, serving as principal coachman to George IV, William IV and, finally, Queen Victoria. How on earth did he find time to fish?

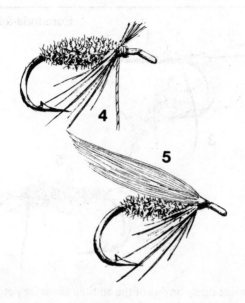

As to the other claimant, in a copy of *The Field*, in the year 1853, there appeared an article which indicated that the inventor of the Coachman was a Kentish angler called John Hughes, who fished the river Cray. But where is old Harding in all this? If any reader can shed a little light on this problem I shall be very grateful.

Certainly the Coachman fly was very popular in the United States and Canada. A variation known as the Royal Coachman was even more popular, the latter pattern being devised by John Haily of New York in 1878.

Let us now tie the original pattern. The hook is usually number 12. Wind the dark green tying silk in close even turns to the bend (1) and there tie in two or three strands of bronze peacock herl (2). Wind the herls over the silk to form the body (3), secure and remove waste. Tie in a bunch of red cock hackle fibres (4) as a beard hackle, followed by two slips of white swan or goose wing feather fibre (5), sloped well back over the body. Complete the fly with a neatly whip-finished head.

Edmunds & Lee

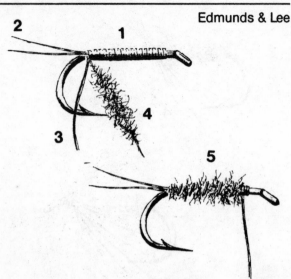

This must surely be one of the all-time favourite wet flies used by thousands of anglers when the natural *Rhithrogona haarupi* puts in its early season appearance. That it is a favourite pattern of so many seems somewhat strange to me because the natural fly is most certainly not evenly distributed throughout the country. I suggest that Wales sees the largest hatches in the early months of the season, with other rivers in the west country and the north having a moderate sprinkling. The common denominator? The rivers where the March Brown is found are usually swift, tumbling waters with rocky beds.

The very knowledgeable angling entomologist, John Goddard, states that the trout will frequently take the hatching nymph in preference to the dun and therefore the artificial tied as a wet fly or a hatching nymph is often more effective. I tend to agree with him.

The natural is quite a large fly, with speckled fawn wings and a body of a dark brown colour with pale yellow rings. Many are the artificials that have been devised down the years to represent this insect. In fact Courtney Williams in his *Dictionary of Trout Flies* lists seven,

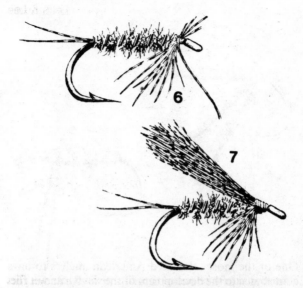

plus six derivatives, and there are many more. My personal preference is for a March Brown described in Edmunds' and Lee's most collectable book *Brook and River Trouting* (1916). I should point out that in Courtney Williams' book he includes a March Brown from the Edmunds and Lee stable, but for some reason omitted this particular pattern.

The hook size I usually use is between 12 and 14. Take the orange tying silk in close even turns up the hook shank to the bend (1) and there tie in two strands of partridge tail feather fibre (2). Now tie in a length of yellow tying silk (3) and dub the original tying silk with sandy coloured fur taken from near the base of the hare's ear (4). Wind the dubbed silk along the hook shank to form the body, and rib it with the yellow tying silk (5). Secure and remove waste dubbing material. Tie in a bunch of greyish-brown fibres from a partridge back feather (6), followed by a wing made from partridge tail-feather fibres of a greyish hue (7). Complete the fly with a carefully tapered whip-finished head, neatly varnished.

33   Grey Hackle

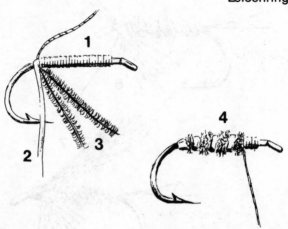

One of the most celebrated American anglers to have contributed to the development of the wet fly, and in particular to the best method of fishing the wet fly, was James Leisenring who lived between 1878 and 1951. A resident of Allentown, in the state of Pennsylvania, his fishing was carried out on the famed Little Le High river, the nearest thing to a chalkstream that our American cousins can hope for, and also on the well-known Brodheads.

Leisenring was a most observant and enquiring angler who spent many hours checking the stomach contents of his catch and making copious notes and sketches, later to be changed into highly successful wet flies and nymphs. He had one oft repeated piece of advice: 'You must tie your fly and fish your fly so that the trout can enjoy and appreciate it'. His attention to detail is shown by the way he would dress the same pattern with hackles of varying degrees of stiffness. Why? Because he wanted stiff fibres for swift, tumbling waters and soft fibres for more tranquil streams, being a firm believer in hackles 'working' in the water. A soft hackle in a swift stream becomes a clogging mess around the body.

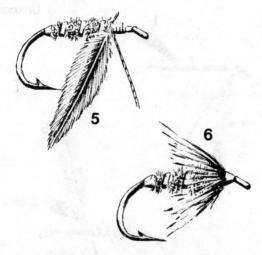

Another Leisenring tip which you may find useful when fly-tying is to strip off the lower fibres when preparing a hackle. He habitually stripped off more fibres from the side of the stalk that is to lie next to the shank. Using this method the first turn or two of the feather beds very neatly. I thoroughly recommend it.

His fishing techniques are also worthy of study. Those of you who think that the 'Induced Take' was devised by the late Major Oliver Kite should read Leisenring's book *The Art of Tying the Wet Fly*, first published in 1941. For more information about this fascinating angler and his methods I modestly suggest you read the chapter about him in my book *Famous Flies and their Originators*.

Now to one of Leisenring's favourites, the Grey Hackle. The hook size is 12 to 14. Take the primrose tying silk in close turns to the bend (1) and tie in a length of narrow gold tinsel (2), followed by two bronze coloured peacock herls (3). Wind the herls to form the body and rib with the tinsel (4). Secure and remove waste. Tie in a creamy or yellow Badger hackle (5) and wind on the hook (6). Complete with a whip-finish, ensuring that the hackle fibres have a laid-back aspect.

Unknown

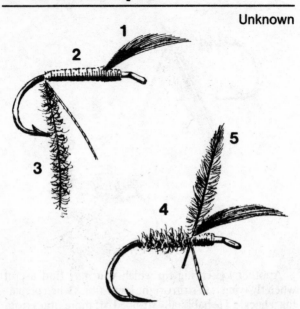

I have on my library shelves a book that I treasure above all others. It is a copy of *A Quaint Treatise on Flee's and the Art of Artyfischall Flee Making*, edited by W. H. Aldam and published in 1876. The book is quite beautiful, with its dark green binding and gold blocking. However, the fascinating part lies in the twenty-five actual flies let into sunken mounts, surrounded by the required fly-tying material. All are perfect examples of flies tied to gut.

Of the twenty-five examples in the book my favourite is the Small Caterpillar. I have used this fly consistently all over the country to great effect, but let the originator speak from the pages of the book:

Comes about 20 May and continues until later end of June. They are a small land bred flee with a single wing of a very light Dun, the Wings lies flat upon the back, the Bodey and Leggs are complately black, the are much in shape and Cise and come at the same time as the black

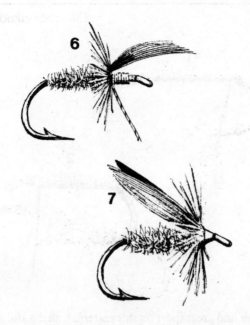

Gnat, and thought by some Old Angler to be the same
flees, but when examined they are found to be quite different flee. One is Land bred, and the other a water bred
flee, and the catterpiller is of short dewration. You may
depend the Catterpiller is a Bluidy killing flee dewring
there short stay upon the water . . . the fish are verrey
fond of them and will have no dennial.

I have often wondered why he called this obviously well-
known natural a Small Caterpillar. But now to the tying
of his pattern. Having placed a number 16 or 18 hook in
the vice take the black tying silk for three or four turns
down the shank and there tie in starling feather wings (1).
Continue the silk to the bend (2) and tie in a length of
black ostrich herl (3). Wind the herl to form the body (4)
and secure. Now tie in a small starling neck feather (5)
and wind behind the wings (6). Pull back the wing
through the hackle and secure. Complete with a small
whip-finish.

Edmonds and Lee

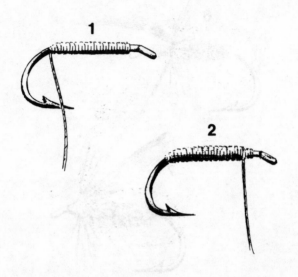

I have had great sport on this pattern. Call it a fluke, or what you will, but on my visits to fish the Hodder, particularly, I have tremendous fun with it, usually when fishing upstream. I'm a great believer in confidence in a fly being half the battle and I have bags of confidence in this one.

Some years ago I tried to discover the origins of the Broughton Point, after being spurred on by Courtney Williams' reference to it having been invented by a Penrith cobbler called Broughton around the year 1830. Williams went on to say that Broughton was a well-known angler who made regular visits to Ullswater. I spent three days in the area trying to find some reference to this old shoe-maker but discovered nothing, except that the beer in Penrith is very good!

The dressing I like best is that described in Edmonds' and Lee's *Brook and River Trouting*. It is of interest to note that in his original book, *Trout Flies: A Discussion and Dictionary* (1932), Williams gave the identical dress-

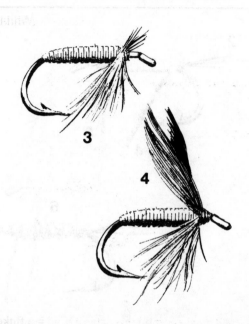

3

4

ing for the Broughton Point as Edmonds and Lee, yet in the first edition of his *Dictionary of Trout Flies* (1949) he had changed the silk from claret to ruddy purple, and the hackle had sprouted a few 'red strands intermingled'. I much prefer the original tying and so we shall get down to it.

The hook size is usually between 14 and 16. Take the claret tying silk in close even turns down the hook shank to the bend (1), and then return up the shank to form the body (2). Tie in a bunch of black hen hackle fibres as a beard hackle (3). Secure and remove the waste. Now tie in the wing slips taken from a starling primary feather (4), ensuring they adopt an almost vertical stance; also keep them quite slender. You can, of course, tie them in at an earlier stage of the dressing sequence as shown for previous flies. Why did I not draw it thus? I can only plead brain fatigue because after thirty-four illustrations my mind is somewhat addled!

Williams

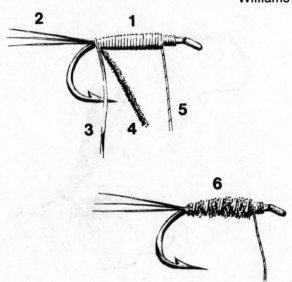

The Williams family seem to have cornered quite a market so far as flies and their histories are concerned. When considering the Broughton Point on the previous page I made reference to books by Courtney Williams; here I am describing a fly devised by his father, Alfred Williams.

Williams senior devised this fly when fishing the river Dysynni and, for over sixty years, he found it to be more successful than any other pattern of wet fly. His son is on record as saying that his father must have taken thousands of trout and sea-trout on it and that he, the son, had always looked upon the fly as his own 'fail me not' standby from May to September.

I must confess that I do not see it as a fly for all seasons, or all rivers for that matter. I have over the years given it a fair trial on all sorts of waters under many different conditions and I have found it to be a far better still-water pattern than a river fly. It could be that ques-

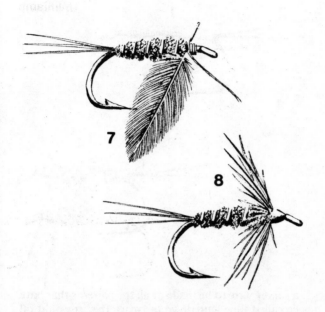

7

8

tion of confidence again; however, the pattern has a rightful place in this book as a firm favourite of a well-known angling family.

To tie the Williams' Favourite is quite simple. The hook size can be what you care to make it, depending on what you may be fishing for. Place the hook in the vice and wind the black tying silk in close even turns down to the bend (1), where you should tie in three black cock hackle fibres as tails (2). Now tie in a length of narrow silver tinsel (3) and a length of black wool (4). Here I should explain that the original pattern had a body made entirely of tying silk, but I do believe the wool body improves the fly. The choice is yours. If you do use the wool, wind the silk up to point (5) and then wind a neatly tapered wool body, ribbed with open turns of the silver tinsel (6). Tie in a black hen hackle (7) and wind in the usual manner round the shank. Complete the fly with a whip-finished and varnished head.

37 Blue Dun

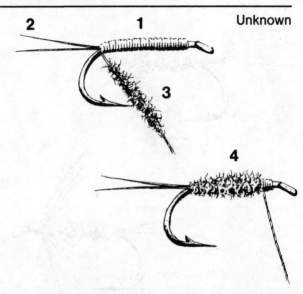

If a survey were to be made of all the patterns that have been called Blue Dun down the years, the list would fill this book. Certainly the Blue Dun was known to Charles Cotton who collaborated with Walton on the fifth edition (1676) of Izaak's *Compleat Angler*. In fact, John Waller Hills in his book of 1921, *A History of Flyfishing for Trout*, suggests that the Blue Dun of Cotton may well be the Second Dun Fly described in Dame Juliana Berners' famous *Treatise*, thereby pre-dating Cotton by one hundred and fifty years. If Hills is correct then the fly was a recognised pattern even before the good Dame put quill to parchment.

Certainly Cotton's fly would be easily recognisable to-day, with its body of bluish-black downy hair combed from a black greyhound, but what of Berners' fly? 'The body is of black wool, the wings of the blackest drake, and the jay under the wing and tail'. Hills asked the question, 'What is the meaning of a jay under the wing and tail?' Is it a jay feather run palmer fashion? Long have I thought about such matters, without conclusion.

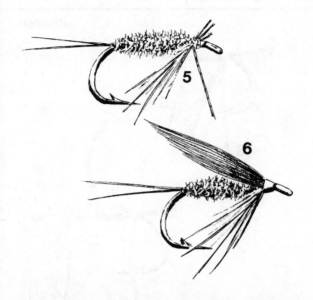

But back to the present day. The Blue Dun dressing is still a firm favourite with many flyfishers who wish to represent olives in their wet or dry forms. Certainly there are many days when we desperately need a good representation of a member of the olive, and the sub-surface pattern that I always tie is the one described here. Do not ask me who first tied it, for I know not. I do know it was one of the first flies that I learned to tie and as such has always been my favourite.

The hook is 14 or 16. Take the yellow tying silk down the shank (1) to the bend and there tie in two rabbit whiskers, well splayed out (2). Wax the silk and dub very sparingly with water rat fur (3), so sparingly that the colour of the silk shows through. Wind the dubbed silk to form the body (4).

Tie in a beard hackle of blue-dun hen hackle fibres (5) and, after removing the waste ends, tie in two wing slips of blackbird primary feather fibre (6) so that they slope backwards at about thirty degrees. Complete the fly with a neatly whip-finished head.

81

Johnson

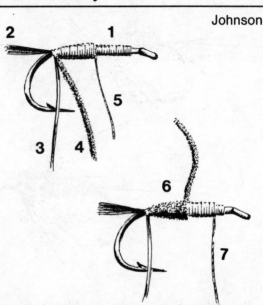

Back in 1972 I had some interesting correspondence with Peter Deane, that very good professional fly-tyer, about the histories of various patterns. One that we covered was the Camasunary Killer, a wet fly that has become one of Deane's most sought-after dressings.

The pattern came to Peter Deane's attention when one of his regular customers, Mr Francis Williams of Melrose, Roxburghshire, sent him the dressing in 1961. It is almost certain that the fly was first devised by Stephen Johnson of Jedburgh, whose family owned the Camasunary fishery located in the Isle of Skye, and who wrote that very entertaining little book *Fishing from Afar* that was first published in 1947.

First and foremost the Killer is a sea-trout fly, Peter Deane having confirmed to me that one of his tying accounted for twenty-one sea-trout and two grilse in one day's fishing! It says a lot for the pattern, but possibly even more about the durability of a Deane-tied fly.

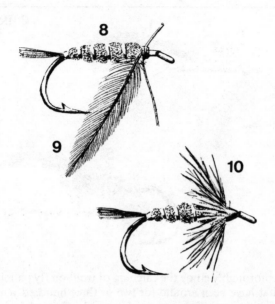

Since I first heard of this fly I have used it in waters far removed from where the sea-trout run and yet it has proved most effective. Certainly rainbow trout of still-waters think it is fine fare, while scaled down on smaller hooks it has proved equally attractive to small brown trout of the border country.

The tying is not difficult. Take the tying silk (I usually use primrose) down the shank (1) and at the bend tie in a tail of royal blue wool (2). Now tie in a length of oval silver wire (3), followed by a length of royal blue wool (4). Wind the silk forward for half the length of the body (5) and wind the blue wool over the silk (6). Secure and remove waste. Tie in a length of red D.F.M. wool, bring the tying silk to point (7) and follow with the red wool. Secure. Rib overall with the tinsel (8). Tie in a long-fibred black cock hackle (9) and wind in the usual manner (10). Finish off the fly with a neatly tapered and varnished head.

Cotton

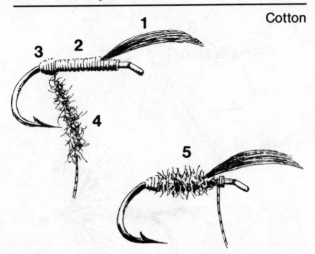

I thoroughly enjoy the catching of trout on fly patterns that have been around for two or three hundred years, and the Ant Fly is a good example. Termed by old Walton's friend, Charles Cotton, as 'a most killing fly' it was one of sixty-five patterns that he described in the 1676 edition of the *Compleat Angler*.

Some present day flyfishers may think that Cotton's flies have little relevance now, but that is far from the case. In fact I would be quite happy to fish for the rest of my life with perhaps a dozen of Cotton's flies. That way, I'm sure, would lead to boredom but I doubt if my annual take of trout would be much reduced, if at all, by the lack of modern flies. I hasten to add that I am now referring to stream fishing, not the chasing of monster still-water rainbows.

But back to the Ant Fly and the pleasures of fishing such old patterns. If you are a lunatic like myself, you will go to the extreme of tying the fly on eyeless hooks bound to fine nylon in place of gut. I would use gut if only I could locate a good source; however, nylon is all right, but do make sure it is well whipped to the shank. I confess that I do not go the whole hog and use a sixteen foot

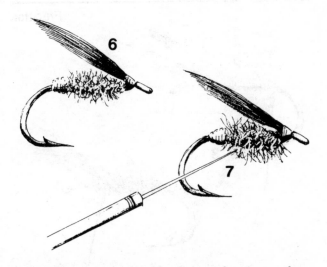

rod without a reel, but it is truly great fun to reproduce
these old patterns just as they were tied so many years
ago, doubly so when you get into a good trout.

The tying is quite easy on modern hooks and, while
Cotton did not specify a particular size, I have generally
tied this pattern on number 14. Start the red tying silk in
close even turns, tying in a slip of rolled primary feather
from a starling's wing (1) as you wind down the shank to
the bend, trapping under the silk the waste ends of wing
material (2). At the bend return the silk back up the
shank for four or five turns (3). Now wax the tying silk
well, and if you would follow to the letter Cotton's instructions you must dub it with the black-brown hair of
a cow (4). Not everyone has access to one of our bovine
friends and so I suggest seal's fur dyed the appropriate
colour. Having dubbed the silk, wind onto the hook
shank to form the body (5). Pull back the wing fibre (6)
and complete the fly with a whip-finished head. Take a
dubbing needle and carefully pick out some of the body
hair to simulate legs (7). Now hands up those who
thought no-hackle flies were recently invented in
America?

Francis

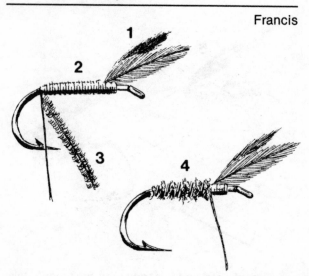

In one's life there are many 'firsts' that stay in the memory: the first day at school, the first girlfriend, the first day in the armed forces and one's first fishing book. The author of such a book usually becomes a hero in the eyes of the novice angler and so it was in my case when I bought a very dog-eared, broken-spined copy of Francis Francis' *A Book on Angling*, fifth edition, 1880. What a treasure trove it was to me and between its battered covers old Francis and I fished for many species on countless rivers. Naturally my favourite fly had to be the Francis Fly. Here is what my old mentor had to say about it: 'I first found it to kill well in the Welsh rivers, where I tested it severely against the far-famed coch y bondu and in whatever position it was placed, whether as stretcher or dropper, it killed above three fish for one killed by the coch y bondu . . . since then wherever I have gone I have found it an unfailing resource when many other favourites have failed. Dressed large it kills sea-trout well, and it has even slaughtered many a lordly salmon; while I have seen large numbers of it, dressed like some huge moth, sent out to India to kill the mahseer amongst the

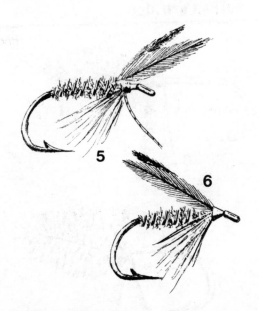

Himalayas'.

What novice could resist a fly that would capture both brown trout and mahseer! Here was the magic touchstone without doubt. I fished the fly with enthusiasm and it worked for me, again a question of confidence I'm sure. Over the years I have neglected this once-loved fly, though the writing of this book has made me resolve to use it again next season. I wonder if the old fish-taking magic will still be present?

For trout I suggest a hook size between 12 and 14. For mahseer I would not even hazard a guess! Start the copper-coloured tying silk down the hook shank and quickly tie in two grizzly blue-dun cock hackle points for the wings (1). Continue the silk in close even turns down the shank to the bend (2) and there tie in a length of bronze peacock herl (3). Wind the herl to form the body and rib with the tying silk (4). Tie in a beard hackle of medium blue-dun hackle fibres (5) and then bring back the hackle point wings (6) and complete the fly with a neatly tapered and varnished head.

Price

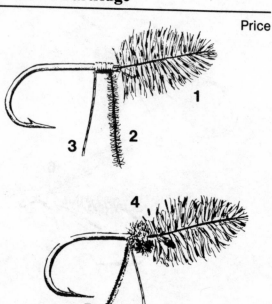

Here we come to one of the few traditional style wet flies to have been devised in recent years, though as Taff Price is quick to admit, it is more a variation on a theme than a completely new design. One wonders if a totally new wet fly need ever again be invented, for the thousands of patterns down the ages must surely cover all our requirements.

Having said that it is possible to gild the lily and Price, a knowledgeable angler and entomologist, has taken a long hard look at such traditional patterns as the Partridge & Orange and the Snipe & Purple and has, to his own satisfaction, effected an improvement to these old flies. In a letter to me Taff called the old northern wet patterns 'Yeoman flies'. What a perfect description! Solid, sound, the backbone of English wet fly fishing. Price went on to say that he had not attempted to alter radically such patterns, rather he had extended the scope of such artificials by giving the flies a slightly different

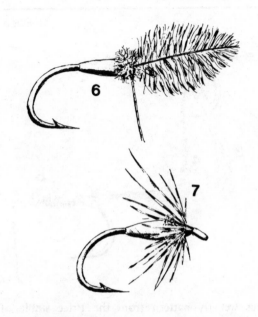

shape with the introduction of a thorax.

Price's Partridge patterns include bodies of white, pink, blue, yellow, orange, hot orange, neon red, green, all fluorescents, plus black, silver and gold. The one constant feature is the partridge hackle.

The fly is usually tied on hook sizes 16 to 10. Larger sizes have proved most effective for sea-trout. The appropriate coloured tying silk is started down the hook shank, at which point a brown partridge hackle is tied in (1), immediately followed by a length of peacock herl (2). The silk is now wound down the shank for approximately one third of its length. Wind the peacock herl to form the thorax (4). Tie in a length of the required body wool (5) and then wind down the shank and up again to form a short body (6). Tie in, remove waste and bring the silk in open turns over the thorax to the front of the hackle. Now wind the hackle, two or three turns only (7), and complete in the usual manner.

Price

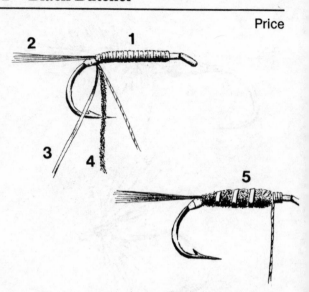

Another wet fly pattern from the Price stable of thoroughbreds. I first came upon this fly back in 1970 when reading John Veniard's good book *Reservoir and Lake Flies* which was published in that year. At the time I was carrying out some experiments with all-black flies, relieved lightly with silver. Price's pattern suited my experiments well, namely to fish for at least half a season with nothing other than all-black wet flies and nymphs, in the hope of determining if shape and size were more important than colour.

In Veniard's book Taff Price recalls how, fishless and in total desperation one hot still day in August when fishing Grafham, he tied his Black Butcher to his point and cast into the flat calm surface alongside the dam wall, retrieving slowly the while. In short order he hooked a trout that when landed weighed over three pounds, and a stomach content investigation showed the fish to be full of snails and precious little else. Price considers that the success of his fly is because when wet it takes on the silhouette of a snail.

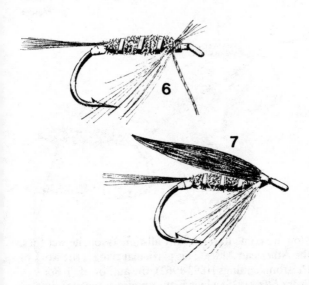

For my part I have found it to be a consistently good pattern when fishing lochs and rivers in the north, and it has been equally productive on still-water locations in the Midlands.

My favourite hook size for this fly is between 10 and 14. Take the black tying silk in close even turns down the hook shank (1), and just round the bend make a tag of flat silver tinsel. Now tie in tail whisks, somewhat longer than normal, made of black cock hackle fibres (2), followed by a length of flat silver tinsel (3) and a length of black wool (4). Wind the wool to form a tapered body and rib with the silver tinsel (5). Remove waste end and secure. Tie in a beard hackle of black cock hackle fibres (6), followed by two wing slips of black crow (7) tied well down and extending to the bend of the hook. Complete the fly with a neat whip-finished head and a coat of varnish.

I am sure that in larger sizes this pattern would make a very good sea-trout fly and I would welcome a report from anyone who puts this pattern to such use.

Jennings

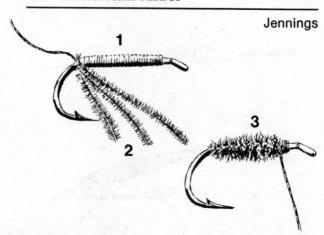

Now we come to one of my all-time favourite wet flies, the American Alder. This particular tying is the work of Preston Jennings (1893-1962), the author of *A Book of Trout Flies* (1935) which in my opinion is the most important entomological/fishing book published in America prior to the 1939-45 war.

When considering flyfishing in America, one must remember that we in Britain had a few hundred years start on our transatlantic cousins. In fact it was not until 1916 that an American book appeared which attempted to relate natural flies and their artificial counterparts. It was called *American Trout Stream Insects* and was written by Louis Rhead. Unfortunately Mr Rhead discarded the recognised scientific nomenclature of fly life and dreamed up his own names for the insects, thereby causing subsequent confusion and rendering his work virtually useless to those future anglers who would relate his artificials to known naturals.

Preston Jennings' book had the same impact on American flyfishing as Ronalds' *Fly Fishers Entomology* had on British angling in 1836. Jennings spent countless hours studying the natural insects of the eastern seaboard and translating what he saw into fur and feather. In his attempts to view the fly from the trout's point of view he

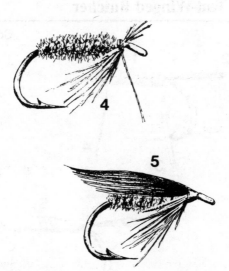

built a special water tank in which to examine naturals and artificials. However, after some months he resorted to a glass prism which he claimed gave the same optical effect.

Space forbids more details about this man and his fascinating work, but for those who would know more I suggest they turn to my book *Famous Flies and Their Originators*.

Jennings' tying techniques were not revolutionary but he did possess an eye for matching material to achieve just the desired effect. To tie the American Alder, place in the vice a hook sized between 10 and 14. Take the claret tying silk in close even turns down the hook shank to the bend (1), and there tie in two or three strands of bronze peacock herl (2). Twist the strands together and wind round the shank to form the body, followed by the tying silk as the rib (3). Jennings used a separate piece of ribbing silk of a rusty-red colour, but I have found this to be an added complication.

Now tie in a beard hackle of hen coch y bondhu (4), followed by two slips of black duck wing feather fibre (5) lying well back over the body, penthouse style.

93

Collyer

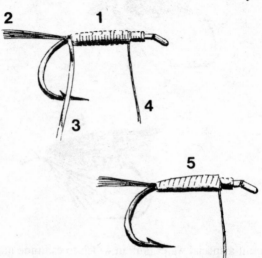

I wonder what it is about the Butcher that makes fly-tyers want to modify the pattern? So far we have examined the original Butcher, followed by Taff Price's Black Butcher and now we come to David Collyer's Teal-Winged Butcher. I could also have included the Bloody Butcher, the Gold Butcher and the Kingfisher Butcher – favourites, I am sure, of many anglers. Why have I singled out Collyer's variant? Two reasons: one, because Collyer is a highly skilled practitioner who knows what he is about, and the other is that shortly after I learned about his fly I tied up a few prior to a fishing trip to the north because I was curious to discover how the trout of a small loch to the north of Glasgow would react to this variant. If this were a film script I could report that the fly killed hundreds of trout. It isn't, and the fly didn't! In fact, over the three days the wild trout were only interested in a Peter Ross and various spider dressings. On the day I came back south I gave a few Teal-Winged Butchers to my local friend who had shared the fishing with me. Back home I

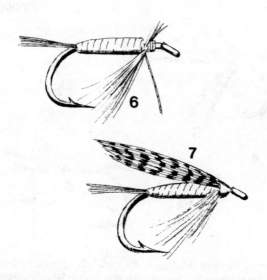

forgot about the episode until a few weeks later when I received a letter pleading for me to send some more of those 'wee b — s with the silver body and teal wing'. Apparently my friend had been doing great slaughter with the fly on other lochs further north. Subsequent fishing trips to that area have certainly proved it to be a very good fly, not that it works every time, of course – such a fly would be terribly boring – but it does its job often enough to ensure it a home in my fly-box.

The tying is quite easy, but do take care when winding the tinsel body. I have seen so many flies spoilt by 'humpy' winding of tinsel. Take the tying silk in close even turns to the bend (1) and there tie in a tail of ibis substitute (2), followed by a length of silver tinsel (3). Wind the silk back up the shank (4). Wind the silver tinsel to form a neat body (5), tying in and removing waste. Now tie in a beard hackle of black hen hackle fibres (6) followed by two wing slips of barred teal feather fibre (7). Complete the fly with a whip-finished and varnished head.

Woolley

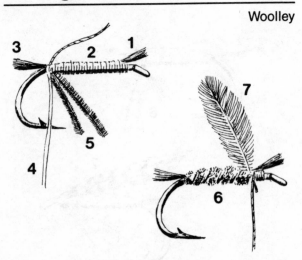

One of the best Midlands fly-tyers who operated from before the turn of the century was Roger Woolley. Born in 1877 at 13, Burton Street, Tutbury, Derbyshire, Woolley rapidly developed a passionate interest in all aspects of angling, not least the manipulation of feathers and fur to reproduce artificial trout flies. However, it was not until the year 1896, when he went to Ireland as a coachman to some gentleman, that he really developed the fly-tying skills which were to ensure his place as one of Britain's greatest fly dressers. I have for many years tried to find out who taught the craft to Woolley when he was in Ireland, without success.

Between 1897 and 1898 he returned to Hatton, Derbyshire, setting up in business as a fly-tying hairdresser. How odd that so many top-line fly tyers have also been either hairdressers or tobacconists. Woolley's skills as a busker of flies soon became known in the Midlands and he rapidly built up a large number of customers who appreciated a Woolley tie.

He did not slavishly follow existing patterns, unless requested, but preferred to base his aritificials on the living insects. His skills were fully recognised when G. E. M.

Skues wrote in his book, *Nymph Fishing for Chalk Stream Trout*, that 'tackle dealers in general, wholesale or retail, with few exceptions, of whom Mr Roger Woolley and Mr T. J. Hanna of Moneymore, Co. Derry, are bright examples, make little effort at genuine representation of the natural nymph'. Praise indeed.

Books written by Woolley are now collectors' items, particularly his *Modern Trout Fly Dressings* (1932); a second edition was published in 1939. His *Flyfishers Flies* of 1938 is equally collectable. Blessed with good health Woolley lived on to the age of eighty-two, tying flies up to but a few days before his death in 1959.

Here I describe his favourite grayling fly. The hook is between 14 and 16. Start the pale blue tying silk down the shank and tie in a switch of red floss (1). Continue the silk to the bend (2) and tie in another piece of red floss (3), followed by a length of fine flat silver tinsel (4) and a pale blue heron herl (5). Wind the herl around the shank to form the body, followed by open turns of the silver ribbing (6). Tie in a pale blue hen hackle (7) and wind in the usual way (8). Complete the fly with a varnished whip-finished head.

Wright

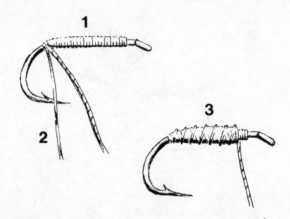

With this fly I really do feel that I am repeating myself *ad nauseam*, for I hate to think of the number of times I have written about this artificial and its history. Readers of my *Famous Flies and Their Originators*, published by A & C Black in 1972, will be fully acquainted with the life history of Jamie Wright, and those who have read my previous book *Fifty Favourite Dry Flies* will have read a truncated version of the history of the Greenwell's Glory.

If it so happens that somewhere in the world lurks a flyfisher who does not know the story of Canon Greenwell, James Wright and the famous fly then I write these pages for him alone. For all others I suggest they skip these two pages and go to pour themselves a large whisky and water before picking up the threads again with the Waterhen Bloa on the next page.

In May, 1854, William Greenwell, a prelate of Durham Cathedral, had been fishing the river Tweed and had had a lousy day. The trout were not taking what the good Canon had to offer them and he trudged back to James Wright's cottage totally fishless, but carrying an example of the natural fly that had proved so attractive to the trout. History does not tell us what the natural was but I think it is a safe bet it was one of the olives.

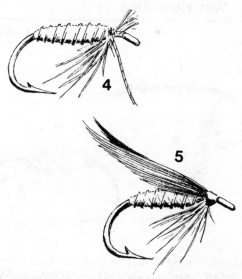

Wright busked up a few artificials, supposedly copies of the natural, and the next day Greenwell creeled a full basket of trout. A party was held that evening to celebrate the event and the local schoolmaster christened the fly the Greenwell's Glory. Rather a pretty story, don't you think?

But did Wright really invent a new pattern on that May evening in 1854, or did he pass on to the Canon a fly known on the Tweed for many a year, one that was devised by a fellow called Mark Aitken which had a pattern that is uncannily like the Greenwell? A fruitful field for the historian.

But now to the wet Greenwell's Glory. The dressing is quite simple. Hook size is generally 14. Well wax the yellow tying silk with brown wax to give it a pale olive colour and wind down the hook shank (1). At the bend tie in a length of fine gold wire (2). Wind the silk back up the hook to form the body and rib in close even turns with the wire (3). Tie off and remove waste. Tie in a bunch of coch y bondhu hackle fibres (4), followed by wings of blackbird wing feather fibre (5). The original pattern had a bunch of fibres split in two by the tying silk. Complete the fly with a neat whip-finished head.

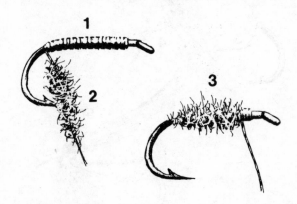

A pattern beloved of many a Yorkshire Dale fisherman
and one whose origins I would love to know. The late W.
H. Lawrie in his book *A Reference Book of English Trout
Flies* (1967) put forward the view that the Waterhen Bloa
had in fact the same dressing as the Blue Dun of Ronalds.
It is unusual for such a careful researcher as Lawrie to
make an easily checkable error, but I just cannot equate
the Blue Dun in my 1862 edition of Ronalds' *The Fly
Fishermans Entomology* with the Waterhen Bloa. For example, the Bloa has no tails or wings. The only similari-
ty I can see is in the body dubbing of Ronalds' second
Blue Dun; he indicates that the fur of the rat, mouse,
mole or rabbit can be used. The true Waterhen Bloa is far
more specific, stipulating fur from the water-rat, as laid
down by Pritt in his book *Yorkshire Trout Flies*, published
in 1885.

T. E. Pritt's book, and the subsequent 1886 version
that was identical in text but had a title change to *North
Country Flies*, is now a much sought-after volume com-
manding a high figure whenever a copy appears on the
second-hand market. Pritt, for many years honorary
secretary of the Yorkshire Anglers Association, produced an excellent book containing eleven plates illustrating
in hand-painted over-wash sixty-two sparsely dressed

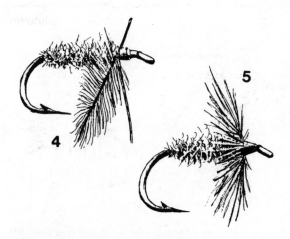

north country artificials.

I am sure that the Waterhen Bloa was in use hundreds of years before Pritt, no doubt taking Yorkshire trout when old Izaak Walton was 'nobbut a lad', but proving such a claim is a different matter. If any reader has views on this matter I shall be delighted to hear from him or her.

F. M. Walbran in his book *Grayling and How to Catch Them*, published in 1895, gave Pritt's dressing, which we are about to tie, but also stated that he had capital sport with the same fly except that the body was changed for one of dyed yellow quill. For interest sake I fished alternate days for grayling with both patterns. Well, the grayling must have changed their feeding habits since Walbran's day because the true Waterhen Bloa took far more grayling, as it has done trout for as long as I have used this excellent pattern.

And now to the vice. Hook size is usually between 16 and 14. Wax the tying silk with clear wax and carefully wind down the hook shank (1). Dub the waxed thread sparingly with water-rat fur (2) and wind to form the body (3). Tie in an inside feather from the wing of a water-hen (moor-hen) (4) and wind round the hook (5). Complete the fly with a whip-finished head.

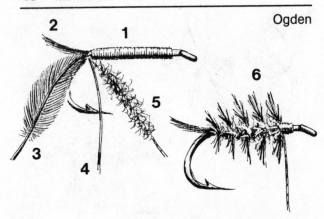

The name of James Ogden who lived and tied flies during the mid to late nineteenth century has already been mentioned in this book, and reference has been made to his own delightful volume *Ogden on Fly Tying* (1879) which is greatly valued by bibliophiles of angling books.

The invention of the Invicta can be laid squarely at the door of Ogden and for many years it was a great favourite of countless flyfishers. That it seems to have dropped out of favour down the years does not detract one iota from its trout-taking abilities, and I would suggest that the Invicta is heading for a revival.

Courtney Williams in his book *A Dictionary of Trout Flies* indicated that the fly was one of the most reliable patterns for lake fishing and went on to say that in northern England it was sometimes used as a river fly. Frankly, I have always thought of it first and foremost as a river fly, especially in the Border areas where it has taken heavy baskets of fish. Over the past few years the Invicta has enjoyed a growing popularity with quite a few regular stillwater anglers who frequent the Midland locations.

Though originally devised as a true wet fly, it requires little alteration to turn it into a cracking floating pattern, one that has given me a lot of enjoyment when fished as a sedge. I recall fishing a beat as a guest a few years ago on a rather exclusive stream where most of the members

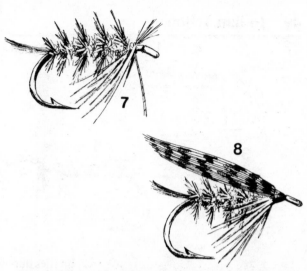

seemed old enough to have been around when Halford was a lad. It was dark by the time I arrived back at the fishing hut where my host and four members were well into their third or fourth large drink. With, I hope, due modesty I thumped down on the table five very good trout to polite murmurs of congratulations. 'What fly?' I was asked. 'Invicta', I replied, then very quickly showed them my floating version to prevent the onset of cardiac arrest among these oh so dry-fly anglers. Alas, all but one of those charming folk are now on the other side of the river Styx.

But now to tie the wet fly. The usual hook size is between 10 and 14. Take the yellow tying silk down the shank (1) to the bend and there tie in a tail of pheasant topping (2), followed by a red hackle (3) and a length of gold tinsel (4). Re-wax the silk and dub wth dyed yellow seal's fur (5). Wind the dubbed silk to form the body, followed by open turns of hackle. Now rib over all with the gold tinsel (6). Secure and remove all waste. Tie in a throat hackle of a mixed bunch of red hackle and blue jay feather fibres (7). Leaving out the blue jay seems to have no effect on the fly's efficiency. Tie in, sloping well over the body, two slips of hen pheasant tail feather as the wings (8). Complete with a whip-finished head.

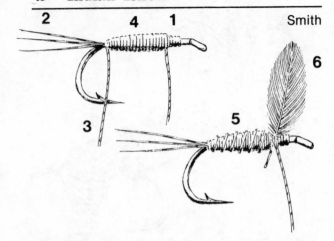

Smith

We are now fast approaching the end of this book and so I hope I may be allowed a little whim, a fly that, if tied strictly to the instruction, will have most of you ferreting around from now until kingdom-come for the required materials. The fly is also of interest because a certain person was accused of 'pirating' it.

It is fair to say that the Indian Yellow, surely a representation of the blue-winged olive, was devised by James Smith of Sharrow, near Sheffield, around the year 1840. W. H. Aldam, who gave us that most collectable of all angling books, *A Quaint Treatise on Flies and Fly Making* (1876), states on page 73 of his book that 'the fly was first brought to my notice more than thirty-five years ago'. He also goes on to say that he used no other point-fly on any river from the middle of May until September. Now that *is* a favourite fly!

The Indian Yellow gave Aldam cause to rail against those he considered had pirated the pattern, being especially scornful of the editor of the fifth edition (1856) of Ronalds' *The Fly Fishers Entomology*, a gentleman who hid behind the pen name of Piscator. Aldam wrote in his book: 'I do not know who edited the fifth edition [I could have told him, it was Barnard Smith] but therein the fly is pirated. The information given to the editor

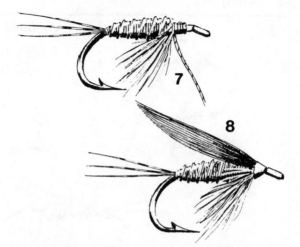

must have been given by one or two 'friends' of mine, perhaps both, to whom only I described the colour of the body as that of new Russian leather, ribbed with fine silk'. Obviously old Aldam was very annoyed and no doubt his two 'friends' got the rough edge of his tongue.

But now to the fly that caused so much bother. Obviously the original was tied to gut but it fishes equally well on a modern hook, I suggest 14. The tying silk is the colour of the afore-mentioned new Russian leather, a light fawnish-red shade, waxed with clear wax. Wind the silk down the shank (1) to the bend and there tie in the tail fibres (2). You may choose from a rich buff coloured guinea pig feather, fibres from a bittern's feather or fibres from a buff Cochin China fowl. Hands up all those who have all three feathers!

Tie in a length of unwaxed yellow silk (3), then return the tying silk up the shank to form the body (4), followed by close even turns of the yellow silk rib (5). Tie in a buff or ginger hackle from a Cochin China hen (6) and wind in the usual manner. Pull the fibres down and back and secure with the tying silk (7). The wings are from the under covert feather of a young grouse (8) and Aldam was most insistent that only a young bird would suffice. Have fun!

Overfield

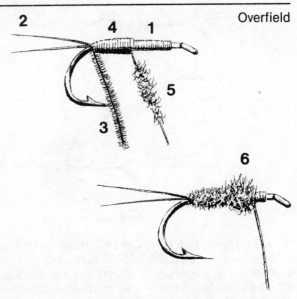

We have now arrived at the last fly in the book and unlike most of the patterns so far described and illustrated this one is not a favourite of countless anglers. In fact, I would lay a lot of money that you have never heard of it, so why is it included as a favourite fly? The answer is simple: it is a personal favourite of my own devising that first felt water on its hackles many years ago after I had tied it while staying in a small Northumbrian hotel.

This pattern has been most useful to me down the years and I have always thought of it as a perfect dual-purpose pattern, being perfectly happy to use it as an up or downstream wet fly or as a nymph when the trout are obviously feeding on such items.

I confess that until I came to write this last chapter the fly never had a name, but for the sake of uniformity it should have one and so I have christened it the Allen Fly, for it was near the East Allen where I first tied it and it was in that river where it caught its first fish.

Since that day it has taken many many trout for me. It has flashed and swerved with the fast moving currents of

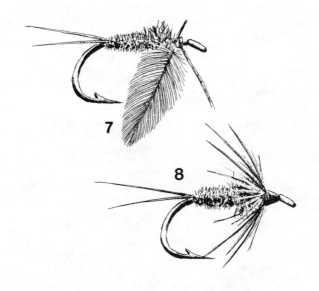

rocky bed rivers, and in its nymphal use has plopped above many a nymphing trout of the classic chalkstreams. I would not claim that it is the answer to all my problems, but its fish-taking record has been impressive enough for me to fish it with total confidence.

The Allen Fly uses no obscure materials or ones which are difficult to obtain and so it is quite within the scope of the merest novice, while the tying is very simple. I always dress the pattern on a number 14 hook. The well waxed purple tying silk is taken down the shank (1) to the bend of the hook and there a tail of pale ginger cock hackle fibres are tied in (2), followed by one or two strands of cock pheasant tail feather fibre (3). Now wind the tying silk half way up the body (4) and wind the pheasant tail fibres over it. Dub the silk with mole's fur (5) and wind over the front half of the hook (6). Remove waste dubbing. Tie in a natural dark red softish cock hackle (7) and wind sparingly in the usual way (8). Complete with a neatly whip-finished head.

Index